Historical Introduction to Anglo-American Law

I0492397

King Edward 1 The English Justinian

J. Stanley McQuade

Preface

This little book is based on a series of lectures introducing legal history to a very interested group of law students at Campbell University Law School. They also asked me to take a class on Roman Law which I did. However, Roman Law is already well provided with excellent introductory books and does not need another one. Legal History on the other hand, while there are superlative large volumes on both English and American legal history, a shorter introductory volume is not easy to find and so I have ventured to attempt to fill the gap. Whether I have done so adequately is another question. If I have stimulated the interest of the reader to take up the larger classical legal history books I will be well pleased. Two very useful works that I have enjoyed and recommended to my class are Theodore Plucknett's CONCISE HISTORY OF THE COMMON LAW and Lawrence Friedman's HISTORY OF AMERICAN LAW.

The founding Dean of the Campbell University Law School, Leary Davis, always insisted that you do not really know the law till you study its roots. Two of the most important of these sources are legal history and Jurisprudence, the study of the great ideas underpinning the law. I have published and taught a great deal in the latter but though I have spent less time in the historical aspect of law I have profited very much, and my students have too, from the time spent in reading up on the history of the Common law in England and America. So as the television chefs say, "enjoy, enjoy.".

TABLE OF CONTENTS

CHAPTER ONE

THE COURTS SYSTEM

§1 *Primitive local courts*

The earliest approximation to a law court that can be found in any society is more like a village meeting. Someone presides and decisions are made by all persons present in accordance with established local custom. Settlement of individual disputes rather than decisions are preferred and if the parties cannot be prevailed upon to come to an agreement due to disagreement as to the facts there is not usually any attempt to hear arguments or consider evidence - the matter is settled by divine test.

This is much the way things were in England after the departure of the Romans in the fifth century. Tribal customs prevailed and local moots did business and heard disputes much in the manner described above. If the facts were not clear resort was made to the ordeal either of water or hot iron and these were rendered more solemn and believable by the presence of the clergy, supported perhaps with some sacred object such as a relic. The result of the ordeal was final and incontrovertible. Increasingly, however, the clergy became unhappy about the ordeal and on occasion are thought to have manipulated it to produce what they thought to be the proper conclusion. The ecclesiastics came to prefer the sacred oath of the party, supported by the oaths of oath-helpers (who swore that they believed the oath taker). Here again the result was final. If one of the parties made their oath and it was or was not supported by respectable oath-helpers, there was no appeal.

§2 *The laws of the Anglo-Saxon kings*

The Anglo-Saxon kings established a measure of central government with the king's household as its administrative center. Some supervision of the local courts was exercised. The King might intervene in a case by means of a letter (breve or writ) and an important case might on occasion be heard before the King himself. The Anglo-Saxon kings also published general codes of laws, such as the laws of Aethelstan, Alfred, Canute and Edward the confessor. The invasions of the Danes in the ninth century allowed Alfred, King of the West Saxons, and his successors to unite the country under a central monarchy but there was still no thought in all this of replacing local custom with a common law. The local customs generally prevailed and the local moots carried on as before. An early twelfth century work entitled THE LAWS OF HENRY THE FIRST (*Leges Henrici Primi*) which is thought to have been written by a continental visitor to England, describes three major sets of legal customs, those of Wessex, Mercia and the Danelaw which were still operative in the early Norman period and so presumably represented the state of affairs in Anglo-Saxon times. The codes likewise merely regulated certain matters, for instance the proper payments (wergild) to accommodate a homicide or the procedure for hot pursuit of criminals or self help or blood vengeance.

§3 *The organization of the Anglo-Saxon courts*

In the eighth or ninth centuries the growing power of the Saxon kings enabled them to modify the traditional social arrangements into forms more suitable for maintaining order and good government. The old vill (village) remained, consisting usually of a number of people who lived in one place and cooperated in the business of farming and otherwise making a living. Such a community was usually centered round a church like the small rural parish which was used as an administrative unit in later Elizabethan times. But although the vill might have its meetings and even courts after a fashion, the really important Anglo-Saxon governmental unit was the hundred. It is not certain exactly what the hundred was. Some have said that it was a taxation unit representing a tax base of a hundred hides. More likely it was a group of a hundred families divided into groups of ten (tithes). Members of the tithe were in effect insurers of one another and were expected to keep one another in line. Failure to control any member created liability to fine or some other penalty by the group. The hundred held a moot every month at which business was transacted and disputes heard and resolved. The ealdorman (reeve) of the hundred presided but did not render judgement, the doom was decided by all members present. This (and not the jury) was the "judgement of one's peers" mentioned in Magna Carta. Twice a year the county sheriff (shire reeve) toured the hundreds (the sheriff's tourn) to hear criminal cases and also to transact business of various kinds on behalf of the king. The sheriff would for instance make sure that everyone was in a tithe and might hold a weapontake to check the readiness of the adult males for military service.

It was required of every free male person in the community that they should render suit in the appropriate local court, and it was considered an onerous duty rather than a privilege. People sought to avoid this burden by obtaining the right to be represented by someone else, and a grant of land or some interest in land might be given on condition that the grantee would attend court as the representative of the grantor. The body of the vill and hundred courts thus came to be largely occupied by serfs and the representatives of the vill and hundred in the county court would tend to be those lesser free men who were required to attend by their more important neighbors and associates. This was one of the reasons why the customary courts progressively declined in importance while the business of the Royal courts expanded. However, local courts (especially borough courts) continued to function until relatively modern times especially in relation to actions in debt.

The united Anglo-Saxon kingdom was divided into counties (shires) many of which represented the old separate kingdoms (Wessex, Sussex etc.). In the more remote border areas of the country new shires were organized round a fortified town called a borough and in these the name of the county and of its principal town were the same. The county and its reeve (the sheriff) became the most important administrative and judicial institution in Anglo-Saxon England and the vill and the hundred quickly lost most of their real character as courts, being only used to apprehend and hold criminals until they could be tried in the county court before what was essentially the king's justice. Only local business and very minor cases could be decided at the local level. Thus the vill and hundred would be expected to apprehend and hold criminals until they could be handed over to the sheriff for trial. If a crime was committed within their boundaries they would have to show that they had done what they could to find and arrest the wrongdoer (for instance to organize a hue and cry). Failure to meet these responsibilities made the vill or hundred in question liable to heavy fines. The county court was presided over by the Sheriff and the Bishop jointly and ecclesiastical matters as well as civil might be decided there. This arrangement may have derived from the theological orientation of the Anglo-Saxon kings (Alfred studied the Bible before promulgating his code) but it also provided a measure of literacy and kept the English courts in contact with continental legal learning.

The boroughs, besides being the chief town of the county also had a charter (franchise) which usually allowed them to hold courts of their own. These might be held under a tree in the open air and were called all sorts of names such as portmanmoots. If they were held indoors they were known as hustings. The matters considered in such courts were frequently of a mercantile nature, as the towns were centers of commerce and trade. Bodies of commercial custom and law developed in the borough courts which remained adequate for the needs of the business community until the late eighteenth century and beyond. Some of the large borough courts such as those of London were functioning well into the nineteenth century.

The Anglo-Saxon kings (as was mentioned earlier) considered themselves the final arbiters of law; appeals and important cases could be transferred from the county courts to be heard before the King and his advisors in the royal household. This was done by means of a letter (breve) from the king, the prototype of the later originating writ allowing access to royal justice. The royal household was a central governmental unit with administrative as well as advisory functions. The most important officials were the secretaries and financial officers and here we have here the essential outline of the later Anglo-Norman curia regis.

The Anglo-Saxon kings and their advisors thus show a degree of administrative and legal sophistication. The arrangements which they established indeed had promise of developing into a uniform and comprehensive legal system and their inclination was to be in touch with whatever was happening on the continent of Europe. But an event, the Norman invasion, was on its way which would disrupt this development and direct the course of legal development in England along other less orderly and progressive lines. Opinions differ as to the result. The great legal historian Sir William Maitland was of the opinion (and many agree) that the Norman invasion was a barbaric intrusion on this promising development from which we have only begun to completely recover in modem times. However, a large body of opinion both in medieval and modem times felt that the separation of English legal development from that on the continent was a fortunate accident which resulted in a superior product. But all parties to this debate agree that the Norman invasion and its sequelae produced far reaching changes which at least encouraged and made possible the peculiarities which distinguish common law countries from those which trace their legal origins to the civil law of Rome.

§4 *The effects of the Norman conquest*

The Normans had no developed legal system of their own to import and impose on England, they were illiterate warriors with no great interest in law as such. Duke William claimed to be the rightful King of England under the will of Edward the Confessor rather than by conquest and announced that he had no intention of interfering with the laws and customs of his new subjects. Nevertheless the doom of Anglo-Saxon law was sealed at the conquest. It was fated to be crushed by a number of policies and arrangements which arrived along with the new rulers.

(i) The military feudalism which the Normans imposed in England produced manorial courts which were substituted in many cases for the vill and hundred and which competed for business with the county courts.

(ii) It was the policy of the Norman and the Angevin kings who followed them, to centralize government and so they systematically reduced the powers and functions of the sheriff. It was inevitable then that the local and county courts, the legal realm of the sheriff, would be reduced in scope and importance.

(iii) While Duke William was an enthusiastic supporter of the Church he was not about to allow ecclesiastics to interfere with government. He immediately decreed that the bishops and ecclesiastics should remove from the county courts and transact their own business separately. The seeds of future conflict between Church and State were sown here but this measure had other legal sequelae. The ecclesiastics were the repositories of learning in the middle ages and this included legal learning, for Canon Law, which was modeled on Roman Law was already well developed in the twelfth century. Their removal from the county courts therefore not only reduced the latter in importance and deprived them of spiritual authority, but separated them from the educational and legal resources of the Church which might have allowed them to speedily produce a comprehensive and humane legal system.

(iv) Finally the Normans tended to settle serious legal differences not by the oath or ordeal but by the barbaric method of trial by battle. This was largely replaced in England by jury trial by the end of the thirteenth century but was not formally and finally abolished till the eighteenth century. The New England colonists in the seventeenth century insisted that it was one of the immemorial rights of Englishmen.

§5 *The development of the royal courts*

The Norman and Angevin kings had a gift for administration and they quickly developed the idea of the royal household into an efficient administrative machine. Two important departments soon appeared, the chancery (the secretariat) and the exchequer (the keepers of the king's treasury) both of which effectively became legal institutions and ultimately courts of law. The chancery, originally the office which handled the king's correspondence, began to issue writs initiating and dictating the form of certain actions at law. This had been done as an occasional and extraordinary measure by the Anglo-Saxons. Now it was expanded to cover routinely certain types of legal dispute. These were originally matters where the King was deemed to always have a particular interest. Thus the exchequer, the accounting office which managed the treasury, began to hear cases where the King had a financial interest in the result. Thus if A owed money to B who owed money to the king, the action of debt against A by B might be heard in the exchequer. Furthermore the Norman kings, like their Anglo-Saxon predecessors, could hear appeals from local courts and intervene in other courts; and from this developed a number of courts, e.g. Kings bench, Chancery etc.

§6   Eyres, justiciars and commissions

It was the custom for the Norman Kings to roam about their realm keeping an eye on things, calling in their local officials to give an account of themselves and asking people if they had any complaints about the Royal officers or any other matters which they wished to bring before the King. Since the King was present, complaints were relayed directly, usually in the form of a simple written and signed complaint termed in Latin a billa (bill). Later it became more common for these roving investigations to be conducted by the kings representatives, justiciars, who were given a commission which outlined their powers. The Latin term used to describe these itinerant exercises was *errantes* (wanderings) and they soon became known as eyres. A justiciar with complete power to do all that the King would do had a general commission and would be said to be conducting a general eyre. More particular commissions, such as *gaol delivery* would only allow the justiciar to try all prisoners held by the sheriff, or *oyer and terminer* which allowed him to look into (oyer) and settle (terminer) private disputes or appeals which were ostensibly awaiting the arrival of the king.

The country was soon divided up into six circuits around which Royal justices continually rode to attend to the kings business. In the meantime another group of approximately five justiciars remained in London to attend to the bulk of the business there. This became the court of common pleas. The general populace wanted royal justice because it was speedier and more certain in its results than the local varieties. They did not, however, care for the eyres which tended to impoverish one and all, especially minor officials and townships. Several kings financed their wars on the proceeds of the eyres. Magna carta therefore demanded that the justiciars remain in London and so common pleas was finally and completely fixed in the great hall at Westminster which had been built for William II (William Rufus). The King, or rather his household, continued to hear appeals and other cases. these were said to be heard *coram rege* (in the King's presence or house) and the legal department which developed to hear these cases eventually spun off to settle in Westminster Hall alongside the Court of Common Pleas and was known as the Court of King's Bench. The same justices might work in either of them at first, a justice of the common pleas might well go on a general eyre and one of the King's intimate legal advisers might sit in common pleas. The appointments later came to be separate, but Common Pleas and King's Bench simply operated at different parts of this great hall, clearly visible to one another. The rooms used by the courts of Chancery and Exchequer were adjoining it and could be entered by going up a couple of steps and opening a door. It was therefore easy for these various courts to communicate with one another and when a particularly difficult case arose they could hold a special colloquy to decide what was best to be done. This was usually held in the exchequer chamber and the court of *exchequer chamber* is thus a general hearing by justices of several courts and is not to be confused with the court of Exchequer itself. As time went by these various courts came to compete for business and indeed their operations became difficult to distinguish from one another. This matter will be discussed later when we consider the forms of action at common law.

All this may seem like a haphazard arrangement and in a sense it was. Yet the competition between these courts helped to develop the law, and a common set of remedies, reasonably comprehensive in their scope, gradually emerged. The disorder was taken care of in England by a series of reform acts enacted in the late nineteenth century.

§7 *Manorial courts and courts leet*

The Normans introduced a particularly stringent form of the feudal system into England, designed to furnish and

14

finance an army and protect the new realm. This system did not last very long, less than a hundred years, but its legal arrangements and their consequences were much more enduring and some of them are still with us. Feudal courts in particular still existed here and there in the nineteenth century in England. A feudal overlord had the duty to warrant the estates granted to tenants and to hear disputes relating to such tenures, as when one of these was displaced by another person. But besides disputes relating to feudal estates in land, a local manor could acquire, either by royal grant or in some other way, the right to hear other kinds of case such as those normally heard in the hundred or even the county court. A manorial court with such privileges was known a *court leet*. They could not hear criminal cases but some of these courts became very lucrative. The customary court of the Bishop of Ely (a feudal and not an ecclesiastical court) was very sophisticated and kept elaborate records. A court leet belonging to the Mosely family was purchased by the city of Manchester in the nineteenth century for a considerable sum (in order to get rid of it).

§8 *The meaning of the term common law*

Glanville, writing in the later part of the twelfth century could speak of the common law, by which he meant the rules and procedures followed generally in the royal courts. And this common law was eventually to supersede the older customary and feudal courts. But this process did not proceed according to any grand plan. There was never any royal policy of squashing the older courts, except perhaps briefly in the mind of the lawyer king Edward I. The Norman and Angevin kings wished to curtail the powers of the sheriffs and so stripped the county courts of their importance. They also wished to assert their interest in other matters such as title to land and so steadily bypassed and reduced the importance of the manorial courts. But the development of the royal courts and royal remedies was a piecemeal affair, supplementing the traditional law in certain matters only. Gradually, however, it drew away virtually all legal business from them and they withered and became dead on the vine long before they were officially abolished. However, as was mentioned earlier, the borough courts and some of the courts leet lasted into the present century and were used for instance to deal with commercial debts well into the nineteenth century.

§9   *The effects of the conquest on English law*

This occasional and supererogatory character in the Royal law had a number of unfortunate results. Since the local actions were not really abolished but only supplemented, various courts existed side by side offering remedies for the same kind of case, and this was rather confusing. It also turned out that as the local courts faded in importance, a number of remedies, such as the action for defamation, disappeared with them and were only slowly and incompletely replaced in the king's courts.

This kind of development also occurred in the American colonies. The early colonists were predominantly from the English towns and were more accustomed to borough rather than common law. Much of the ancient procedure in these courts was therefore transferred to the colonial courts and a somewhat tortuous legal development came about in America also. Insofar as the Americas inherited the common law, which they did as a matter of right, they acquired its peculiarities such as the effects of the royal writ system and determination of matters of fact by a jury of their peers.

All these matters will become clearer as we consider the writ system, the jury and other later topics.

ILLUSTRATIVE DOCUMENTS

Records from the manorial court of the bishop of Ely's Court at Littleport on Tuesday the feast of S. Dunstan in the fourteenth year of King Edward the Second [i.e. Tuesday, 19th May, 1821.].

William Michele complains of John Tepito that he unjustly detains from him 1s and 6d. for a cow and a calf sold to him. And the said John says that he owes him 4s for the said cow and calf, and as to the 7s. 7d. he says that he paid it to creditor the said William by command of the court: and this sum (of 7s. 7d.) is awarded him and as to the remaining 6d. he says that he is bound in no penny of it on the aforesaid sale; and this he at once proved in court by his law, which was coerced him by his opponent (William). And therefore it is considered that William do recieve the 4s. 5 d. and John be in mercy (3d.) for the wrongful detention, and likewise ti William be in mercy (2d.) for the false claim of 6d.

It is found by inquest that John Beucosin wrongfully detains sheaves and oats belonging to Henry Sweetgroom as for the work which he [Henry] did for him [Jo the lord], in breach of covenant, to the damage of Henry taxed at 4d. Therefore it considered that he recover etc., and John in mercy.

William Thame complains of William Abbot (3d.), Michael Gigil (3d.), John Boystons (3d.), Alan Rushpiller (3d.), and John Gigil (3d.) in a plea wherefore they fished in his several fishery to his damage 20 s., and whereof he produces suit
And the said William Abbot and the others come and defend etc., and avow the fishery whereof he complains is common and not several, and pray that this inquired. And the said William [Thame] says that they should not be admitted to inquest, for till he holds the said fishery of the lord by a certain yearly rent in several and thereof he vouches the record of the terrier. And the terrier being inspected witnessed that the said fishery is several. Therefore it is considered that the said William of Thame do henceforth hold the

said fishery in severalty and also do recover against them his damages which are taxed at 30d. and the said William Abbott the others be in mercy; they mutually pledge each other.

Littleport. Court there on Wednesday next after the feast of S. Luke in the year of King Edward the Second.

It is found by inquest that Rohese Bindebere (3d.) called Ralph Bolay thief and he called her whore. Therefore both in mercy. And for that the trespass done the said Ralph exceeds the trespass done to the said Rohese, as has been four therefore it is considered that the said Ralph do recover from the said Rohese his taxed damages.

CHAPTER TWO

THE WRIT SYSTEM

§1   *The forms of action at common* law

The old adage "no writ, no remedy" is not quite true. As the royal writs were extending the business of the royal courts they were not acting in a vacuum. They arose in the background of the customary courts. The royal writs, however, gradually took over more and more legal business especially since, by the writs of *toll* and *pone,* a case could be transferred from customary to royal courts. The royal writs then, each carrying its own elements which had to be alleged and each with its own procedures and defenses, became the basis for much of our modem law. Our causes of action are derived from them so that, as Maitland remarked, "we have buried the forms of action but they rule us from the grave".

§2   *The writs*

A writ is literally a letter, *breve* in latin. Sometimes they were sealed (as when they were directed to an official such as a sheriff. If they were open (the usual case when directed to a private person) they were called letters patent (breve patens). Writs were conventionally divided into *original writs* and *judicial writs.* Original writs (which should perhaps be called originating writs) initiated legal proceedings, directing sheriffs or courts to proceed and try cases. These were normally issued in the chancery. Judicial writs on the other hand were those arising out of legal proceedings and were normally issued by the court in which the case had been heard, e.g. the court of common pleas. A venire facias e.g. might be used to summon a jury, a levari facias to order the seizure of goods in satisfaction of a judgement or a fieri facias to order something to be done (see notes on procedure).

Well known and tried writs were described as *de cursu* writs. i.e. they would be issued as a matter of course and so could be found in one or other of the registers of writs, largish volumes in the fourteenth century. A writ could of course be issued *de novo* by the clerks in chancery and they were indeed supposed to do so if a meritorious case were to appear. Since however the judges in the common law courts could quash such writs and refuse to recognize them it was a rare event for a new writ to be issued by chancery unless suggested or requested by a judge. It was more common indeed to change the rules for an existing writ, expanding its role to cover new cases rather than providing a new one.

§3   *The writ of right*

The first writ of any importance was the writ of right (*breve de recto*). This was originally a Royal command ordering a feudal court to do justice in a certain case. It became important however when Henry II issued an ordinance that no man need answer for his freehold in land without a royal writ (i.e. it became a private right). There is no record of this ordinance but it was assumed to be the law of the land in Glanville's time in 1179. This did not mean that a case could not proceed in the feudal court without this writ but that the defendant was entitled to insist on it, i.e. he had the option of defending in the customary or the royal court. There were various reasons why a defendant might choose the royal court one of the most important being that the plaintiff was his feudal lord. If plaintiff and defendant were the tenants of different feudal lords, Henry II ordered that there would be no choice, the case should be tried in the county court. The writ of right was an order to the feudal court in the form: "do justice in the case of A --- and unless you do so my sheriff of [county] shall do it, that I may hear no more about this matter. Henry II's chancery was very free with this writ and used it to take business out of the feudal courts as the feudal lords may well have hesitated to try a case if the king was interested in it.

When the king was the immediate lord of the two parties, i.e. the dispute concerned land granted directly by the king, then the matter would of course be heard in the kings own feudal court, the council. The appropriate writ here was a *praecipe quod reddat* (order --that he restore). This was a direct order from the King (via his sheriff) to the party complained of to restore the land to the complainant (plaintiff). Henry II however also used this writ in other cases, in short directly ordering a defendant who was not his immediate tenant to restore the right in land. The sheriff had to *return* this writ to the Royal Chancery, together with the names of the summoners who had served it. The feudal barons objected to the removal of cases from their courts in this way and inserted a clause in Magna Carta [1215] to the effect that the writ *praecipe* should not be used to deprive the feudal courts of jurisdiction. This proved an ineffective provision for although a feudal lord could object to the issuance of a praecipe he might well hesitate to do so and in fact most feudal courts permitted the Royal praecipe to proceed. It was particularly appropriate indeed when, as was often the case, the feudal overlord was one of the parties in the case.

§4 *Defects in the writs of right.*

1. How was the issue to be decided. Among the Normans it was decided by trial by battle whereas the English used warranty of law [compurgation]. Later it became difficult to tell who was French and who was English but by then it had long been decided that the grand assize should be available to decide such matters. This was a declaratory jury of 12 knights who would state of their own knowledge and opinion which of the two parties had the right to the land. However, an assize was not available as a right but only as a privilege. It could be requested by one of the parties but the court could and often did refuse to order it. The Royal courts, however, began to order the feudal courts to grant an assize (see Hamo's case) and this was a further reason why, despite the prohibition of Magna Carta, praecipes wee sought by litigants and continued to take business from the feudal courts (see discussion of Hamo's case in Plucknett).

Powerful or wealthy defendants could otherwise obtain better champions and intimidate plaintiffs. In the case of compurgation they might also threaten persons who might otherwise warrant for the plaintiff.

2. It was a very slow remedy. The writ of right was based on very old traditional procedures and essoins [excuses for not appearing in court] were allowed. There were a number of these that were deemed legitimate, one of them, a favorite, being illness. This seems fair but it came to mean that the defendant (warned of a projected visit by a sheriff's officer) could take to his bed and be lying there when the officer arrived. He was allowed to do this for a year and a day. If there was more than one defendant, e.g. joint tenants, they could take ill in turns (a device called fourcher) and the delay was even greater.

§5 *Henry H's reforms - the petty assizes*

Aware of the problems with the writ of right, Henry II "by dint of much loss of sleep" [according to Bracton] developed the petty or possessory assizes. These provided a rapid return to the status quo, with the disseised plaintiff restored to possession pending the result of further proceedings under a writ of right. The defendants essoins and other delays would not then be able to starve the plaintiff into giving up his claim. The most important of these possessory assizes were:

1. *The assize of novel disseisin.* This was a possessory action used when the plaintiff claimed that he had been recently and wrongfully disseised by the defendant. In order to bring his suit he had to show that he had been seised at some recent date [the last harvest in England or within the last year in Normandy] and that he had been wrongfully *disseised* by the defendant. The issue was put to a jury of 12 free men [they did not have to be knights as in the grand assize]. Compurgation and trial by battle were not permitted as alternatives and no essoins were allowed. This was deemed fair since the matter was supposed

to be temporary and real title could be sorted out later under a writ of right.

2. *Mort d'ancestor.* When a tenant died his heir was entitled to be seized by the feudal lord. If the fee was given to someone else the heir could bring a petty assize showing that his ancestor had been seized and that he was the legitimate and proper heir.

3. *Darrein presentment.* This concerned the right to make someone the clergyman in a particular church [known appropriately as a "living"]. The right to do this resided with certain persons, e.g. those who had built the church or otherwise acquired this right. The living could be sold and so was accounted an estate residing in the grantor which reverted on the death of the incumbent clergyman and could then be granted [in return for a sum of money] to someone else. If there was any doubt as to who had the right to present and if this situation lasted more than three months, the bishop concerned was entitled by ecclesiastical law to make his own presentment and thus a loss was sustained by the private persons claiming this right. One who was for any reason deprived to the right to present an ecclesiastical living could bring a possessory assize showing that his family or ancestor had made the last presentment [darrein presentment].

4. *The assize utrum.* This arose when there was a dispute as to whether [lat. utrum] land was held in ecclesiastical tenure [frankalmoigne] or was a true feudal estate. If it was held in frankalmoigne title would be decided in the ecclesiastical courts but if feudal then in the royal courts. If one of the parties was an ecclesiastic or a religious corporation a lay person might well prefer that the matter be heard in a common law court and vice versa. The jury of 12 free men in this case decided whether the estate was ecclesiastical or feudal and the matter tried accordingly.

5, *Aiel, bisaiel,* and *cosinage.* These were actions developed for cases where the ancestor involved in any of

24

the above situations was not the plaintiff's father but someone who was more remote. Aiel was the writ when the ancestor involved was a grandfather, bisaiel for a great-grandfather and cosinage for a great-great-grandfather [three degrees of remoteness being deemed the same as for a cousin.

The question as to the originality of Henry II's possessory remedies has been disputed. Some have argued that it was derived from the *actio spolii* of Roman law which was similarly a swift remedy when someone had been forcefully ejected from their property. Others have argued that though there are resemblances between the two and the king might have taken a hint from them, essentially the possessory assizes were an English remedy for an English problem, certainly the feudal details can be so regarded.

§6 *Developments of the writ of right - writs of entry*

A number of extensions of the writs of right were developed which proved more durable than the originals from which they derived and in fact made writs of right popular remedies. These were known as *writs of entry* and they allowed the plaintiff to enter on the defendants land on the ground that his title was defective and the plaintiff's was not. These were primarily developed in cases of *non-recent disseisin,* e.g. in 1205 the writ *sur disseisin* was evolved to meet the case when the tenant [defendant] was an heir of the disseisor. Later the writ *de quibus* was devised for cases when the plaintiff was an heir of the disseisee. The great thirteenth century justiciar William Raleigh developed a writ called *ad terminem qui praeterit,* whereby a termor of years, whose term had expired, could be evicted from the property. The writ *cui in vita* was used by a widow whose husband had wrongfully conveyed away her dowry during his lifetime. The writ *sur cui in vita,* as one might expect, was brought by her heir in similar circumstances. The writ *in casu proviso* was brought by the remainderman against a widow who had wrongfully conveyed away her dower property [e.g. her life estate in one third of the land had been used to convey the land in fee simple to a third party]. Chapter 24 of the statute of Westminster II (1285) had declared that a writ should be issued in a similar set of circumstances [*in consimili casu*] to those covered by an existing writ but where one was not available as a remedy and the case was otherwise meritorious. Chief justice Bereford [early fourteenth century] after a fierce argument with counsel in a case, cited this statute and demanded that a writ of entry for a remainderman be issued. This writ therefore became known as *in consimili casu.*

§7   *Other developments of the praecipe*

1. Debt/detinue. This action could cover either a debt or a wrongful detention of someone's property (detinue). It is an ancient remedy which generally followed the form and rules of the *praecipi quod reddat,* since the debitor or detainor was ordered to hand over the money owed or the property detained to the plaintiff. It had many uses. It was extensively used In connection with sales (to sue for payment) and it was also used to sue for the return of a charter or deed relating to land. It could also be used against a bailee. It had all the disadvantages of the old writ of right but somehow survived as an available action alongside more convenient remedies. Thus warranty of oath (compurgation) was still available as a defense to an action for debt in certain courts until relatively modern times.

2. Account. Cases of account are found in the year books of the year 1200. It was then available for feudal lords against their bailiffs but, perhaps by some confusion of the terms was also available against bailees generally. It came to be used in partnership cases where one partner could require another to bring in their books and render an account.

3. Covenant. The Statute of Wales (1284) was meant by Edward I, the great layer King, as a comprehensive civil code. It mentions the action of covenant which seems to have been a rather general action covering all sorts of promises express or implied. It could be used for instance to demand the return of a fishing boat which had been borrowed; to enforce trusts (uses); or demand the return of mortgage money, or the thing mortgaged; or to proceed to final concords transferring title to estates in land. Its use for contracts pure and simple declined rapidly when Edward I made it mandatory that for covenants to be actionable they must be under seal. Only the (illiterate) nobles had seals and thereafter the action was very restricted in its scope though it still survives to the present in the form of covenants in a deed.

§8 *Writs of trespass ostensurus quare*

Towards the end of the twelfth century a new group of writs began to appear which were not demands that something be done but rather complaints about a wrong done. In these the defendant was required to show why (*ostensurus quare*) he had done something wrong. The trespass actions developed in this form but were not common until the fourteenth century. The reason given for this is that since they were compensated by money damages and money was rather scarce, jurymen could not be persuaded to travel to London on a fool's errand. With the development of the *nisi prius* system in the fourteenth century (and perhaps the greater availability of money for damages) the action became feasible and popular since the factual aspects of the case could be determined locally and the jurymen did not need to travel to London. Whether these explanations are correct or not, the trespass actions, long available, are only found in the fourteenth century, many of them tried in minor courts before justices of the peace.

Trespass vi et armis. This was noted in the plea rolls of 1249. Bracton proposed to comment on these actions but never got round to it' The essence of the trespass actions was a breach of the King's peace, a wrongful injury for which damages are due. Maitland opines that that these derived directly or indirectly from the appeal of felony where a crime was announced, the criminal denounced and then pursued and apprehended. The appropriate .defense was denial and the offer to prove this denial with the accused's body [trial by battle]. Compensation might indeed be offered especially if the accused had taken refuge in a church. This crude procedure with its likelihood of a bloody contest ensuing was replaced on the criminal side by jury trial and on the civil side by the action of trespass.

§9   *Other trespass actions*

In addition to actions for trespass to the person other trespass actions appeared. These included:

De bonis asportatis. This was developed to cover cases where someone's goods had been removed and the action for trespass to chattels derives from it.

Quare clausum fregit. This means literally that the defendant had crossed the boundaries of the plaintiff's enclosed land and the action of trespass to land developed from it.

Replevin. This was a rather ancient remedy designed to help a tenant whose goods had been distrained by his feudal lord or by the sheriff (to induce him to appear in court). The plaintiff gave surety to the sheriff that he will appear and court to answer his lord's complaints. Possession of the distrained property is then conditionally restored. The reply by the lord was called an *avowry.* If the avowal is successful the lord would "get the return" of the distrained property. If any question of ownership was raised, an interlocutory proceeding could be introduced called *de proprietate probanda* (concerning proof of property). Later plaintiffs had a choice between *de bonis asportatis* and *replevin*. The choice made depended on technical points which might or might not give the plaintiff an advantage. In de bonis, possession was deemed to lie in the defendant pending the outcome of the action, in replevin it was transferred temporarily to the plaintiff. Replevin is of interest in the history of American law in that it was extended to cover all sorts of cases where goods were wrongfully retained i.e. as a substitute for detinue.

§10 *Trespass on the case.*

This writ has no connection with the famous ch.24 of the Statute of Westminster II (1285) known as "in consimili casu". The action on the case takes its name from the fact that whereas the original trespass actions concealed the real facts of the case under the formal complaint (often untrue) that with "force of arms and spears and axes etc. the defendant had injured the plaintiff or damaged his property". In these new actions the real facts complained of in the case (in casu) were explicitly stated. The old action had the key words "ostensurus quare". The newer ones had an additional clause beginning with the word "cum" (since) i.e. since he (the defendant) has done the following bad things. This action existed in 1368 since it was then ruled that arrest of the defendant was appropriate for trespass but was not allowable in the action on the case. The major difference of course between the two actions was that in the action of the case fault must be alleged. At first either action could be pleaded interchangeably but in the earlier part of the nineteenth century it was felt that they should be distinguished, with each of them providing a distinct remedy to be used in different circumstances. At first they were distinguished by saying that trespass should be used for direct injuries and the action on the case for indirect injuries and this view has lingered long in the case law of a number of states. Around 1830, however, it became settled that trespass should apply to intentional injuries and the action on the case to negligent torts.

§11 *Some developments of the action on the case*

Ejectment. A tenant for a term of years, since he was not invested with a fee simple, originally had few rights against a third party but only a right *in personam* against the landlord. A number of actions were developed to help termors of years but the most effective was an action on the case called *de ejectione firmae* (being ejected from one's farm). This was available by the end of the 15th century and was indeed so convenient that the owners of a fee simple began to use it by means of a fiction. The two parties would each rent the property to two imaginary persons John Doe, , and William Stiles who was interfering with his term of years. The question of title could be settled during the proceedings and this avoided the various disadvantages and delays endemic in the ordinary writ of entry derived from the writ of right.

Assumpsit. This was an action on the case using the words "*ostensurus quare cum assumpsit*" (to show why when he had undertaken to)" i.e. the defendant was required to show why he had undertaken to do something and had not done it. Much of our modem law of contract derives from this action.

Trover. This was an action on the case where the defendant had found something belonging to the plaintiff and had appropriated it to themselves. It was used when goods were being held by one person which were rightly the property of another. The action for conversion of goods derives, though somewhat indirectly, from it.

§12 *Judicial writs*

The final events in a case were carried out by means of judicial writs i.e. writs that issued from the court rather than the office of the chancellor. The defendant might well be declared to be in the mercy of the king (amerced). This meant that he was fined for the trouble to which he had put the Royal courts. No writ was required unless the defendant refused to attend or was unable to pay. In that case he would be arrested and the writ to accomplish this was called a *capias* (addressed to the sheriff with the words "do thou take"). Further results might be that a *levari facias* might be issued on behalf of the plaintiff to seize the property of the defendant until he should pay. Later the sheriff was allowed to sell these goods to satisfy the judgement. If a *fieri facias* was issued the profits (e.g. the crops on the defendant's land) could be taken until the judicial debt was satisfied. The writ of *elegit* (so called as it alleged that the plaintiff had a choice of remedies) was later developed to allow the plaintiff (not the sheriff) to elect either to enter and distrain or to sell in order to satisfy the judgment.

ILLUSTRATIVE DOCUMENTS

FROM THE LUFFIELD REGISTER
[In Cambridge University library]

Writ of right.

1. Edward, by the grace of God King of England, Lord of Ireland, and Duke of Aquitaine, to his bailiffs of B., greeting. We command you that without delay you grant full right to A. de N. concerning one messuage with appurtenances in B. which he claims to hold of us by the free service of so much per year for all service (or *thus*– which he claims to hold of us in free burgage tenure or in frankalmoin) of which B. deforces him; and if you do not do this, let such-and-such a sheriff do it, in order that we may not further hear any outcry thereof for want of right. Witness myself at Westminster the first day of January in [1282] the tenth year of our reign.

n.b. This writ is always patent ; and it should be known that when anyone claims to hold in free burgage or in frankalmoin it ought not to be said "per year" nor "for all service".

1a. The king to ———, greeting. We command you that without delay you do full right to A. concerning so much land with appurtenances, in such a vill, which he claims to hold of you by the free service of so much per year for all service of which B. deforces him. And if you do not do this, let such-and-such a sheriff do it, in order that we may not further hear any outcry thereof for want of right.   Witness, etc.

This writ is always patent. Otherwise concerning the same.

1b. The king to _____, greeting. We command you that without delay you do full right to A concerning two messuages, twenty acres of land, five acres of pasture, twenty acres of woodland, and rent of ten shillings with appurtenances in N. which he claims to hold of you etc., whereof Adam de L deforces him of one messuage and twenty acres of land, B. de D. of five acres of pasture, S. de E. of one messuage and twenty acres of woodland, and J. de A. of rent of ten shillings. And if you do not do this, let such-and-such a sheriff do it. That not further etc.

1c. And if nothing save land only is sought against several, then thus: whereof A. de L deforces him of ten acres, and B. de D. of eight acres of land. And thus let the word "terre" in this case always be put against the last deforciant. Note that the same rule applies when nothing is sought except pasture or woodland or anything similar. If the service be military, then thus : which he claims to hold of you. Here is not said "by free service" or "per year" but "by the service of one Knight's fee, or a half or a third or a quarter part of one knight's fee for all service'. Or thus: which he claims to hold of you by the service whereof so many carucates, or bovates, or hides, or virgates of land make one knight's fee : nor let it be said "per year" nor "by free service". Or thus : which he claims to hold of you by the service of so many pence when forty shillings are taken for scutage **for all service or when** twenty shillings are taken for scutage. Otherwise concerning the same.

ld. The king to _____, greeting. We command you that without delay you do full right to a woman, A., concerning so much land (or concerning one burgage) with appurtenances in N. which she claims to hold of you in free marriage, of which B. deforces ber. And if you do not do this, etc. And it should be known that in a writ concerning free marriage and free burgage and frankalmoin it is not said "per year" nor "for all service".

Otherwise for right.

le. The king to so-and-so, greeting. We command you that without delay you do full right to A. concerning ten acres of land with appurtenances in N. which he claims to hold of you in free burgage (or in free marriage, or in frankalmoin) of which B. de-forces him. And if you do not do this, the sheriff etc. That no further etc. Witness etc.

If. There are, however, innumerable services in the writ of right according as they have been established by different lords; sometimes, however, thus: which he claims to hold of you by the free service of finding for you one sergeant to go with you to the army in Wales at your summons and at your cost (or his own) by the free service of carrying your writs within the Kingdom of England at your summons and your cost within such-and-such a county (or within the Kingdom of England) for all service (or by the free service of one red falcon or one red sparrowhawk or of one pair of gilded spurs per year for all service).

Otherwise for right.

Ig. The king to go-and-so, greeting. We command you etc. --- he land which he claims to hold of you by the service of performing for you what pertains to him in the matter of finding you one cross-bowman to go with you in our army, for all service.

If the land is partable between brothers or sisters, and one deforces many, or many deforce one of his reasonable share, then thus :

The writ of right which is called *de rationabili parte*.

The king to _____, greeting. We command you etc. which A. claims to be his reasonable share which belongs to him (her, or them) of a free tenement which belonged to C. the father (or mother, grandfather or grandmother, uncle or aunt, kinsman or kinswoman) of A., in such a vill, and which he claims to hold of you by the free service of so much per year for all service ; of which B. deforces him (or them). And if you do not do this, etc. that [we may bear] no further outcry etc.

2a. If they have one part and do not have the other part, then thus : which claims as part of her reasonable share which belongs to her (or to them) from a free tenement - which belonged to so-and-so, in the said vill, and to hold of you etc.

And if the land which is demanded is appurtenant to that which **is** held, thus: which he claims to pertain to his free tenement which he holds of you in such a vill by the free service of so much per year for all service etc.

Note against J. to the bailiff for the custodian of the honor of Gifford. To the custodian of the honor.

1. The king to the bailiffs of the soke of such a place (or thus to the custody of such-and-such an honor) greeting. We command you that without delay you do full right to A. concerning so much land with appurtenances, in such a vill, which he claims to hold of the aforesaid soke (or the aforesaid honour) by the free service of much per year for all service, of which B. deforces him. And if you do not do this, That not further, etc.

If the land ought to be held of an heir who is under age and in wardship, then thus: Otherwise concerning the same, to the guardian of the land or of the heir.

1. The king to the guardian of the land and of the heir of C., greeting. We command you etc. which A. claims to hold of the aforesaid heir by the free service of so much per year for all service, of which B. deforces him etc.

The writ of right of dower ought always to be directed to the heir of the husband, or the heir's guardian if he is under age, unless that tenement has come to the hand of the chief lord through default of an heir, and then it ought to be directed the chief lord.

Writ of right of dower.

1. The king to so-and-so, greeting. We command you etc. that you do full ri to A. who was the wife of H., concerning the third part of so much land with the appurtenances in such a vill, which she claims to hold of you in dower by the free service of so much per year for all service (or thus otherwise) : which she claims to her reasonable dower due to her out of the free tenement which belonged to H. formerly her husband in the same vill, (or thus otherwise) : in another vill, and to hold of you by the free service of so much per year for all service, (or thus otherwise) which she claims to be of her reasonable dower due to her out of the free tenement which belonged to H. formerly her husband, in the same vill, (or another) and to hold of you by the free service of so much per year for all service of which B. deforces her of so much, and C. of so much. And if you do not, etc. That no further etc. Witness myself, etc.

False judgment in the county court.
[De falso iudicio]

1. The king to the sheriff, greeting. If A. shall have given you security etc. then cause to be recorded, in your full county court the plea which was in the said county, by our writ of right between the said A., demandant, and B., tenant, concerning so much land etc. whereof the said A. complains that a false judgment had been made against him in the same county court. And have that record before our justices **ete,.** under your seal and by four lawful knights of those who were present at this recording, etc.

False judgment in the court of a lord.

The king to the sheriff, greeting. If A. shall have given you security etc,., then, having taken with you four discreet and lawful knights of your county, go in your own person to the court of so-and-so at N. and in that full court cause to be recorded the plea which was in the said court by our writ of right between the said A., demandant, and B., tenant, concerning so much land with appurtenances in N. whereof the said A. complains that a false judgment has been made against him in the said court. And have that record before etc. under your seal by four lawful men of the said eourt of those who were present at that recording etc. And summon, by good summoners, the aforesaid B. that he be [there] at that time etc. to hear that record. And have there the summoners,, the names of the four men, and this writ. Witness, etc.

To a party that he should not sue.

. The king to A., greeting. We prohibit you from prosecuting a plea in Court Christian about chattels and debts whereof B. complains that you are drawing him into a plea in Court Christian, unless those chattels or those debts relate to a testament or a marriage, because pleas of this kind which do not relate to a testament or a marriage pertain to my crown and dignity. Witness, etc.

Prohibition of waste

The king to the sheriff, greeting. We command you that you do not permit B., who was the wife of H., to make waste, sale, or exile of lands, houses, gardens, fishponds, woods, and men, which she holds in dower from the inheritance of A., to the disinheritance of the said A. Witness, etc.

CHAPTER THREE

THE JURY

§1 *The origins of the jury*

Since the time of Sir Edward Coke, who (on the basis or a rather doubtful interpretation of Magna Carta) interpreted the jury as the constitutional bulwark of freedom from judicial and governmental oppression, the jury and its origins has been a subject of considerable interest to historians. Some have derived the jury from Scandinavian judicial procedures, which are mentioned e.g. by king Aethelred and examples of something like a jury can be found in the Dane law (which survived in pockets of England for centuries). It is more likely however to be a survival of the Frankish royal inquisition. The Frankish kings were wont to question groups of responsible locals with a view to levying taxes. The local inquisition was used by William the Conqueror's commissioners in compiling the Domesday Book. They would gather a body of locally knowledgeable people together to determine what property each person had (in order to tax them) and they also enquired about local customs which they considered relevant. The inquisition was used for the discovery and *presentment of crimes.* The royal commissioner in *eyre* (from the Latin errantes meaning to wander) or *oyer and terminer* (Norman-French meaning to see and deal with) would ask local juries to present to them those accused of murder or theft and these persons would thereupon be tried. This kind of process was also used by Henry II when he developed the *petty assizes* or *possessory assizes* to rapidly reinstate those who had been wrongfully disseized from their property. In these proceedings the factual questions were answered by a jury of twelve free men in the petty assize (which decided e.g.,whether the plaintiff had been recently and wrongfully disseized). A grand assize of 12 knights could decide who actually owned the land.

§2 *The crisis of 1219 a.d.*

Further development of the jury took place after 1215 when in the fourth Lateran council the Church announced that the clergy could no longer take part in or be associated with the *ordeals.* Up till this time it had been customary for courts to settle questions of guilt or innocence, truth or falsehood, by a variety of ordeals. In the ordeal of the iron the person being tested held a hot iron in their hand for a fixed period of time. The bum was then dressed and the lesion examined two days later. If it was clean then they had been telling the truth if not they were deemed to have lied. In the ordeal of the water the person tested was lowered slowly into water until they were immersed over the depth of their own hair. If they sank to this depth the water had accepted them and so their word was true. If they floated, the water was rejecting a liar and their word was false. These ordeals obtained such credibility as they had (in some cases not much) from the presence and activity of officiating clergy. Once the ecclesiastical presence was removed they were simply a lottery. It took some years (perhaps due to communication problems) for this decree to take effect in England but eventually in 1219 a letter was issued in the name of the young King Henry III to the justices in eyre. In this they were advised (since the ordeals were no longer available) as to what they might do in different sets of circumstances. Those accused of serious crimes who were of bad reputation were ordered to leave the country and they should be kept in gaol till it was decided what to do with them. If however they were persons of previously good reputation they should (presumably only if it was likely that there was substance to the charge) be allowed to quit the realm. Those accused of lesser crimes could be allowed to go free and placed on probation pending resolution of the crisis.

§3 *Hamo's case*

Shortly after the provisional arrangements mentioned above were put into effect we find juries being used to determine at least some of the factual questions which came up during trials. In the appeal of felony the proper proceeding (for Normans) was trial by battle but a jury could be asked whether the accusation had been brought out of hatred and malice only *(de odio et aitia). Hamo's case,* found in the plea rolls of the year 1220, is illustrative of procedures in the early thirteenth century. A horse which had been stolen from Hamo allegedly by Phillip King turned up as a plough horse with Edward who later gave it as a marriage present to his daughter. The case was appealed from a baronial court held under the auspices of the Earl of Brittany. This was not a court of record and so four jurors came to swear as to the proceedings there. Trial by battle on behalf of Edward was offered by one Elias Piggun who was probably a professional champion. There were a large number of persons present at the royal assize and the judge, who was none other than the great Martin Pateshull, questioned four juries from surrounding areas. Each gave an independent opinion, not based on any evidence, but relying simply on their own knowledge or even beliefs based on "what everyone said". They had different opinions about most of the relevant questions but all agreed that Elias Piggun was lying. Pateshull remanded the case back to the Earl of Brittany's court but ordered that Elias should lose a foot for perjury, warning him that he had got off lightly. This case illustrates many interesting things e.g. the kind of pleading that was carried on in these early courts. The present feature of note is that this is the first known case where a jury was being asked to settle a question of fact in issue between two litigants.

§4   *The unpopularity of the jury*

Juries in the form of inquests were old but this new use of them was not favored by many and was much criticized. The *Mirror of Justice,* a work written around 1290 describes the jury as being oppressive. Many persons even preferred the old ordeals but compurgation (wager of law) was particularly favored and survived in the common law action of debt and also for other purposes in the borough courts. The great law of London survived long in the borough courts of that city where it was considered a civic privilege and could even be used in cases where citizens of good reputation who were being tried for a felony. In this fearful procedure a large number of warrantors were taken, half from one side of the river and the rest from the other. If even one of these compurgators refused to believe that the accused was telling the truth he was forthwith hanged if the accusation was for a capital crime.

§5   *Prison forte et dure and peine forte et dure*

In view of all this opposition it was at first felt necessary that the parties should consent to it, but means were soon found of coercing them. They could be imprisoned until they agreed and this was known, in Norman/French, as "prison forte et dure". Somehow this was translated into "peine forte et dure" which consisted of laying the accused between two planks and using them to pile rocks on his chest until he submitted. Most no doubt accepted this pressing invitation to a jury trial but those who were guilty and had little chance of an acquittal would sometimes persist until they suffocated under the weight of the rocks in order to protect their families from forfeiture of their property.

§6   *Getting the bugs out of the jury trial*

A number of problems relating to jury trial had to be dealt with. One of these was difficulty in finding a suitable jury for notable persons. A peer of the realm had the right to be tried in the House of Lords by his peers, the high nobility of the land, but the rights of knights were not clearly defined. In 1221 one Thomas de la Hethe, a knight accused of piracy, insisted on a jury of knights and succeeded in getting one: they found him guilty and he was hanged.

There were a number of problems related to the ways in which a jury might acquire the information on which they should base their decision. It was of course desirable that the jury should be drawn from the county where the events in dispute took place. However, the events sometimes spanned more than one county so that a jury from either one of them would be ignorant at least as to some part of the case. It was usual in such cases to allow jurors from both counties to sit together on the same jury. If the jurors felt that they did not know anything about the matter, special jurors, who knew something about the case, could be associated with them to supply information. Juries were permitted to make some enquiries or even to go out of the court and ask questions but no one was allowed to volunteer information to them. Anyone who did so was liable to quite severe penalties.

The boundaries between the various counties were rather uncertain until modern times and some areas in England were not in any county. Events which took place on the high seas were likewise not deemed to be in any county. Exceptions then had to be made (highwaymen could be tried in any county along the road that they used to ply their trade). In the case of crimes on the high seas, the Crown was empowered by statute in the 16th century to select a county where they could should be tried.

§7 *Presenting evidence to the jury*

Panels and juries of various sorts were used to indict people of crimes and the accused naturally objected when their accusers turned up on the trial jury. Since an acquittal might even suggest a false accusation they felt, and with some justification, that members of the presenting jury had a vested interest in seeing that they were found guilty. As late as the mid-fourteenth century objections to jurymen on these grounds were still being refused, perhaps because it was felt that they knew the facts of the case better than others. Eventually, however, when it became the custom to present evidence to the jury even this argument lost its force and the presenting jurors were not allowed to sit in the trial jury.

Accused persons likewise sought to have local persons removed from the jury in case they should be swayed in their opinions by local gossip. A friend of Edward III who was accused of a crime sought by royal influence to have the jurors removed who were from the actual place where the deed was done and this request was denied. At a later date it became proper grounds for the challenge of a juror.

§8 *The unassailable jury*

Wrong decisions by a jury were dealt with by an action for *attaint*. In this the decision of the twelve was itself put to a jury of twenty four persons. It was considered a serious charge and if found guilty the attainted jurors could be fined or even imprisoned. Not unnaturally the second jury would feel some sympathy with the first one and indeed were usually most reluctant to find against them. Consequently this action became virtually extinct and the objections against jury verdicts were instead brought on the basis that the jury had been misinformed or otherwise led astray by those who presented the case to them in court or instructed them as to their duties.

The position of the jurymen was rendered even more secure by the constitutional struggle between the autocratic Stuart monarchy and the growing tide of democratic sentiment in England during the early part of the seventeenth century. It had been the practice of the royal curia to oversee the work of juries and to punish those whom they felt had acted wrongfully or even negligently. The Tudor monarchs were conspicuous in this regard. Queen Elizabeth I in 1544 had interfered in the case of Sir Roger Throckmorton. Throckmorton was undoubtedly guilty but he was a local hero and the jury acquitted him. The queen, however, made them apologize and parade with notices around their necks in Westminster Hall (the central courthouse of those days). The Stuarts attempting the same kind of interference were less successful. The provision of Magna Carta that no one should lose life, limb or property except by the law of the land and the judgement of his peers was interpreted by Sir Edward Coke in a manner that made trial by a free and uncoerced jury a constitutional right (despite the fact that the jury as we know it did not exist when Magna Carta was written). In Bushel's case the Chief Justice, Vaughan, laid it down that the royal prerogative had no part in policing the jury. He went further and claimed that such oversight was in any case unnecessary since they were already open to review by the action of attaint. This was a specious argument since the action of attaint, as has been mentioned earlier, was no threat to the jury. The truth of the matter was that the jury was now seen as a bulwark that was needed to protect the ordinary citizen from the hand of government and officialdom. Vaughan's view therefore prevailed and the jury, except for obvious malice, is essentially unimpeachable.

§9 *Modern criticisms of the jury*

The jury has recently come under fire from other directions. In criminal trials involving terrorists or organized crime it is not easy to protect juries from undue influence. In civil trials on the other hand it has been claimed that they greatly add to the length and complexity of trials and that where jury trials are the rule, insurance rates, e.g. automobile insurance rates, go up. In the United Kingdom civil juries have been abolished since 1987 (except in certain special circumstances e.g. defamation and cases where fraud is alleged). They have also been suspended in Northern Ireland in criminal cases involving terrorists (Diplock trials). In short the jury is currently a live topic in law and one that cannot be discussed properly without some understanding of its history.

ILLUSTRATIVE DOCUMENT
HAMO'S CASE

Philip, Hervey's son, Robert, Humfrey's son, Henry, Andrew's son, William Richard's son, four free men of the court of the Earl of Brittany of Cheshunt, summoned to make record of battle waged in their court between Hamo Moor, the appellor, and Elias Piggun the appellee, touching a stolen horse, whereof Hamo makes appeal, come and record that Hamo Moor complained in the Earl's court against Philip King, for that he stole a mare of his in his common pasture wickedly and in felony and in larceny, in the peace of God and in the peace of his lord the Earl, and this he offered to prove by his body on the hour of the day as the court should consider. And Philip came and defended wickedness, felony and larceny and said that he had a warrantor and would produce him in due season, namely, one Edward; and a day was given him to produce [Edward]. Then Philip, after casting three essoins, came and produced Edward his warrantor, and Edward took up the warranty of the mare. And when Hamo saw [Edward] seised of the mare, he counted against him by the same words that he bad used before, adding that he knew no other thief than Edward whom he saw there in seisin and who had taken on himself to warrant the mare; and he offered to prove against him by his body etc. And Edward defended all of it word by word, and vouched to warranty Elias Piggun, whom he produced. And Elias took hold of the mare and took up the warranty and said that he sold the mare as his own proper chattel to Edward. And when Hamo saw Elias seised of the mare, he counted against him, and said he knew no other thief than Elias whom he saw there in seisin and who had taken up the warranty against him; and he said that wickedly and in larceny, in the peace of God and of the Earl, Elias stole the mare, using the same words as before; and this he offered to prove by his body etc. as the court etc. And Elias defended all of it word by word and offered to behave against Hamo as regards the mare as though it were his [Elias's] own proper chattel, as the court should consider. It was thereupon considered that Elias should give gage to defend himself and Hamo gage to arraign.

And Hamo says that [the four recorders] do in part record well, but in part too little, for when Elias vouched to warrant and warranted the mare to Edward, [Hamo] challenged him as being a hired champion, whom Edward had hired for money to become his warrantor, and of this [Hamo] produced sufficient suit; and that this [account of the proceedings] is true, he now proves by one who saw and by another who heard, and if this be not enough, he offers the king one mark for an inquest thereof; for he says that he could not get this [challenge] allowed him, though he craved that it might be allowed.

And the said four [recorders] on behalf of the [Earl's] court say that the record is as they record and not as Hamo says; and that it is as they record they offer to deraign by the body of a free man of the court, or as the [King's] court shall consider, or to defend that the record is not as Hamo says as the court shall consider.

And Elias being asked where he got that mare, says that before the war she was given him at Cardiff in Wales together with some pigs, by a certain man in consideration of lessons in sword-play, and that he possessed her for six years, and brought her from Wales into these parts, and sold her to Edward for three shillings and a penny, outside Waltham at the cross. But as to the sale he produces no suit, but confesses that he and Edward were alone together. And Edward says the same. Edward also says that he has had the mare these five years.

And Hamo says that the mare was foaled to him, and that he still has her mother, and that she was stolen at Easter in the third year of the reign, and of this he has sufficient suit.

47

And Elias , being asked how he knew the mare after so long and interval says that he knew her by a mark, namely a slit in her ear.

And eight of the men of the vill of Cheshunt, and as many of the vill of Waltham and of Wormley and of Enfield, are summoned to certify the justices.

The following are pledges to produce Elias Piggun Monday before [Mid] Lent; Thomas of Mutton, Peter of Nereford, and the four knights who brought the record.

A day is given them to hear their judgement, on Monday before Mid Lent, and then let them come without their armour. At that day they came, and Elias is committed to the Fleet gaol by the king's council.

Hamo's pledges to prosecute; William the Tanner of London and John of Hale.

Eight men of Waltham being sworn say upon their oath that, as they believe (for all the countryside says so), the mare was foaled to Hamo, and that it was taken in the common of Cheshunt, and that Hamo found her in the plough of Philip King, and that Edward had given her by way of marriage gift with his daughter to Philip; and that after this action had been begun in the court of Cheshunt, Philip handed over the mare to Elias Piggun, the would-be warrantor, in order to enable him to swear safely; and they say positively that in no other way did the mare ever belong to Elias, nor had he brought her into those parts. They add that, as they believe, the mare went in Philip's plough for two years, and they rather think that Edward had taken her from the common by mistake and in ignorance, and not in the manner aforesaid [i.e. not in felony].

The men of Cheshunt being sworn say that they know not whether the mare was foaled to Hamo, but they rather think that she was not; but they know well that Edward gave her to

Philip as a marriage gift in manner aforesaid, but they do not believe that Elias ever sold her to Edward; but they know well that in the presence of the whole parish of Cheshunt, Elias said that he [took up the warranty] for God's sake and asked all men to pray for him so truly as true it was that he did this for God's sake and not for lucre; and so they believe rather that he did it for God's sake than for any other cause. As to the marriage portion of Edward's daughter they have heard nothing.

The eight men of Wormley being sworn say that they know not whether the mare was foaled to Hamo, but they know well that Edward gave her as a marriage gift with his daughter to Philip; and they believe that Edward bought her, they know not from whom but they do not believe that Elias had ever sold her to him.

The eight men of Enfield say upon their oath that they well believe that the mare was Hamo's and foaled to him, for all men say so, and that Edward gave her as a marriage gift as aforesaid, and they know well that Elias never sold her to Edward, but [Elias] has [taken up the warranty] for money, to wit, for ten marks whereof, as they believe, he has had five marks and five are still due to him. And some of them say that they think that [Elias] has done this to get Edward's daughter to wife as well as the money.

Cognizance of the case between Hamo and Edward is restored to the Earl of Brittany by the king's council and they have leave to compromise, and let Elias have his judgement in the king's court. It is considered that he do lose his foot, and be it known that by the action of the king's council he is dealt with mercifully, for by law he had deserved a worse punishment.

Thomas of the Heath, taken on an indictment for thefts and other misdeeds and for receipt [of felons], comes and will not put himself upon his country. The jurors say upon their oath that they suspect him of the receipt of Hobbe Golightly, who was a known thief and was afterwards hanged at Campden, and of this and other thefts they suspect him. And twenty-four knights chosen for the purpose say the same as the said twelve jurors, things. Therefore let him be hanged.

CHAPTER FOUR
PROCEDURE

§1 Self help.

The right to take the law into ones own hands was curiously much more limited in earlier and cruder times when people generally were inclined to proceed in this way. In more settled times when people had become more likely to seek legal redress the law could afford to be more lenient in this regard and allow reasonable self help. However, In Bracton's day persons dispossessed of their land were expected to use a possessory assize rather than to eject the intruder themselves. Also, before seizing someone's chattels to compel them to do what was right, all sorts of formalities, including leave of a court, were required before their goods could be distrained. Eventually distraint could only be carried out by the sheriff and other officers appointed by the court. There were, however, some recognized exceptions. If someone was committing a minor infringement such as would not justify arresting him, his coat or some other personal item could be taken to induce him to appear in court. Similarly animals which are causing destruction of property can be seized and kept until the damage is made good. Any harmful agency could likewise be distrained, the item being known in law as *damage feasant* (*damnum facientem*) i.e. the thing which is causing harm. Early in the thirteenth century it was recognized that a landlord could, without consulting any court, distrain the goods of a tenant who had not paid rents or performed services. This is thought however to stem from the fact that as lord he is exercising the powers of his own manorial court. Nevertheless the lord was still quite limited in what he could do. Certain animals, e.g. those used for ploughing, could not be taken and the lord could not use the animals in any way himself. He must be ready to produce and show them at any time and must return them to the tenant if gage and pledge are offered. If he refuses to return them on offer of gage and pledge, the sheriff can be asked to deliver them and use all necessary force to do so. The hue and cry can even be used when there is refusal to return distrained property once gage and pledge have been tendered. Such refusal was termed *vetitum namii* (vee de nam) and considered tantamount to robbery.

Before the end of the thirteenth century most of this procedure had been replaced. Either party could have the cause removed to the royal courts and the action of replevin (replegiare) was being developed. This was because refusal to return distrained property in the appropriate circumstances was considered (like robbery) to be an offense against the king's peace.

§2 *Procedure*

This term really covers two subjects, *mesne process,* the means whereby a defendant was induced to appear in court or otherwise comply with the demands of the law. *Court* procedure also described the rules governing pleading and proof.

Criminal procedure might be minimal or nonexistent where the killer was caught red-handed or (in the case of a thief) *hand having.* If the hue and cry pursued a thief or murderer they would bring them before a hastily convened court and they would be hanged or mutilated or whatever forthwith without the right to be heard. *Infangthief* was the right to hang one found hand-having within the boundaries of the manor while *utfangthief* allowed execution of one caught outside the court's jurisdictional boundaries. This kind of summary criminal procedure was frowned on by the royal courts and reviewed so stringently that it gradually disappeared and was replaced by indictment and trial.

Where criminal charges were brought against anyone either by private appeal or by sheriff and/or vill, the accused would be arrested and held. If they could not be found they would be declared *outlaws.* This was a terrible event, for being outside the law meant that you had no rights of any kind and could be murdered with impunity. It also meant that all the outlaw's property was forfeit. If outlaws were captured they were hanged merely on showing their outlawry, without considering the offense for which they were outlawed.

It was usual following arrest for prisoners to be released pending trial unless there was great risk of them taking flight or where the charge was very grave e.g. treason or homicide. In the twelfth century even treason and homicide were repleviable. The accused was handed over to some person or persons who undertook to deliver him for trial, or he could find persons who would give pledges that he would appear. This was termed replevin (*replegio* in Latin) and by the thirteenth century. a writ *de homine replegiando* could be obtained *de cursu* (simply by asking for it without fee) which required the sheriff to release the prisoner to the *plegii* unless he was imprisoned by the command of the King or for some unreplegiable offense. The pledges originally laid their hand on the prisoner's shoulder to indicate that they were taking charge of him and this taking in hand (*manucaptio*) was termed *mainprise* in Norman French. Prior to the conquest (in Normandy) the mainpriseurs were termed the Duke's living prison and if the accused was allowed to escape were subject to the same penalty that he would have suffered if found guilty (which probably included forfeiture for a felony). By the twelfth century this impossible burden was reduced to loss of chattels only and fixed bailment amounts became common. It was usual indeed to release a man to the *tithing* in which he was enrolled and they would be responsible for a fixed amount of bail if he should escape. As the tithing system broke down it became more difficult to get out of jail pending trial until the development of the professional bail-bondsman who operated much as they do today.

An alterative defense to mainprise or bailment was to claim that the charge had been made out of hatred and malice and a routine (*de cursu*) writ *de odio et atia* was available for this purpose. Yet even if the accused prevailed with this writ against their accusers and was released without bond, the crown still had the right to make them stand trial so that they could be arrested at any time. There was indeed little protection for the citizen against the crown in the early days of the common law. The thirteenth century judges were really administrative officers and the servants of the crown whose duty was to do the monarch's bidding. It was an unusual event when the great thirteenth century judge Sir William Raleigh declared that the outlawry of Hubert de Burgh by royal proclamation had been unlawful.

One accused (unless taken red handed or hand holding) would normally respond by a denial of the charges. This was indeed the original meaning of the term defense (*defensio*) in the legal context. The only defense originally would have been in the form of a *general denial* but later (as we shall see) special forms of pleading called *exceptiones* were permitted (e.g. I killed him but it was in self defense). The court would then put the accused to the proof which meant trial by battle against their accuser or else submitting to the ordeal (of which more later). By the early thirteenth century however it was possible to purchase from the court the privilege of an enquiry (*inquisitio*) by one's countrymen. This was the early original of a jury trial where a body of the neighbors declared what they knew or honestly believed about the charge. This is the *trial by one's peers* mentioned in Magna Carta (see Chapter on the Jury). Courts were suspicious of both ordeals and oath-taking as means of establishing guilt or innocence and quickly came to prefer the local enquiry (see report of Hamo's case, decided in 1221, appended to the previous chapter). Even when judgement *per iudicium dei* was permitted, its efficacy had become suspect both by church and state. Statistical studies of old records have suggested that at least half of the accused went free and in some areas all were declared innocent. Henry II in the Assize of Clarendon c14 (mid twelfth century) therefore commanded that if the accused were of doubtful reputation (e.g. having got off on previous occasions) that even if the water accepted them or the burn healed cleanly they should abjure the realm.

In continental Europe and in countries which adopted the civil law tradition, the device of the *inquisitio* did not lead to the jury and eventually developed into judicial inquisition where the judge makes the enquiry and determines guilt or innocence.

§3 *Sanctuary*

A person who had committed or was accused of committing a crime could take sanctuary in a church. Any consecrated building would do for this purpose and the accused would be, temporarily at least, beyond the reach of the law. It was then the duty of the four neighboring vills to surround the church and prevent the accused from escaping. The coroner then came to parlay with the refugee who had two main options. He could submit to trial or abjure the realm. In the latter case he left the church in pilgrims garb and made his way speedily to a port appointed by the coroner. He forfeited his lands and chattels and was henceforth an outlaw who would be hanged forthwith if he returned to England. If after forty days the refugee had not decided on either of these alternatives the coroner would order him to be starved out. The church considered this an invasion of its sanctuary rights but in most cases an agreement was reached and prolonged siege was not needed. England was indeed able to export a considerable percentage of its criminal population to Europe by this means.

Sanctuary is no longer with us but its end product, abjuring the realm, is alive and well. State courts in America have discovered that by making discharge contingent on leaving the state tey can hand the criminal over to the authorities in some other jurisdiction.

§4 *Civil mesne process*

Getting the defendant into court in a civil case could be a very difficult matter because *mesne process* had a long history in Germanic customary law and many of these customs, intended to ensure fairness, made for delay. Bracton describes the series of events, like the slow tightening of a screw, that were intended to induce the defendant to make an appearance. These were:

Summons (by sheriff or summoners)

Attachment by pledges

Attachment by better pledges

Issuance of habeas corpus for their appearance

Ceremonial distraint (merely *declaring* the defendant's goods to be *in manu regis*)

Distraint to prevent the defendant from using the articles

Grand distress (the sheriff accounts for profits to the crown

Exaction (arrest) or if this was not possible

Outlawry.

At each of these stages the defendant might have a valid excuse (*essoin*) and so not be adjudged contumacious. He might indeed have several opportunities to respond at each stage, a protection considered necessary because of poor communications and the difficulty of travel. The old Germanic law was very reluctant to adopt the two obvious measures that might compel attendance, i.e., to attach the body of the defendant and to give judgement by default. Gradually however both of these things were introduced, though still hedged about with exceptions. Thus even when, after several non-appearances, judgement for land was given by default to the plaintiff, the defendant could always bring an action to recover it using a higher writ. Thus a writ of entry would be superior to a petty assize and a writ of right to a writ of entry. Following judgement by default on a writ of right indeed the defendant could bring a further writ of right (an equal writ) in hope of recovering provided this was done within a reasonable time.

In actions for trespass *vi et armis,* since these were quasi-criminal causes, an arrest could be made following failure to appear. The judicial writ for this was called a *capii respondendum* with outlawry if it should fail. The outlawry declared here was termed minor *outlawry* (like the minor excommunication of the church) and did not involve a sentence of death. In these actions *imprisonment on mesne process* became the main weapon used by courts against contumely defendants. This may be one of the main reasons why in so many actions where there had clearly been no force or arms involved the offense was nevertheless deemed to have been carried out with bows and arrows or stones and spears and brought as trespass *vi et armis*. Thus a bailee of some casks of wine who had drunk from them and replenished them accidentally with salt water so that the wine was spoiled, was sued in trespass, the writ claiming that the deed had been done with bows and arrows etc.. The improvement in *mesne process* in trespass actions indeed caused most actions at law to be brought in this form. *Quare clausum fregit* was used for trespass to land and later trespass actions for leaseholders *(quare ejecit infra terminum) came* to be the usual actions for deciding title to land while *assumpsit* became the main form of action for breach of contract.

§5 *Final process*

It is commonly thought that specific performance was invented by the chancellors developing equitable relief to supplement the common law. However, this is not so. In the twelfth and thirteenth centuries judicial writs were likely to order seisin of land or goods rather than money damages. They could also command a lord to cease demanding services or a tenant to perform them. In short specific relief was the rule at common law rather than the exception. The parties might be required to give pledges that they will do as the court requires or a curator may be appointed to see that they do so, e.g., where a life tenant had been commanded to cease from committing waste. The commonest case where moneys were awarded would be in actions for debt and remedies which allowed money damages were developed in debt cases. As commerce developed it became more and more important that debts could be speedily and conveniently collected. The *fieri facias* allowed the sheriff to make up the amount of the debt from the defendants goods (sparing work animals and essential tools *etc.*). *Levari facias* allowed the debt to be levied from the fruits of the land but the land itself could not be touched (since the debtor in early times was tenant rather than owner and other persons had interests in it). By the Statute of Westminster II (1285) the writ of *elegit* was devised which allowed the successful creditor to elect between a fieri facias and a new procedure which allowed him to take possession of one half of his debtor's land until the debt was satisfied. Edward I indeed went further than this and in his Statutes Merchant allowed the creditor to demand seizure and imprisonment of the debtor's body until the debt was paid. Borough and staple courts had similar remedies as one would expect, since commerce would be seen as preeminently important in such places.

Damages did not usually include legal costs which in the case of actions concerning land (requiring a sergeant at law) could be considerable. There were a few exceptions to this such as when a tenant attempted to defraud his lord of incidents such as wardship. Roman and ecclesiastical law were kinder to the winning parties in this regard, following the principle *in expensarum causa victus victori condemnandus est* (to the victor belongs the spoils).

§6   *Pleading and proof in civil cases*

In manorial and local courts pleading would normally have been oral and followed fairly strict customary forms. Many of these forms were also followed at first in the royal courts and they have left their imprint on civil procedure even down to the present day. English law writers, when law books came to be written, often classified actions after the model of Roman Law, speaking of real and personal actions etc. Legal practice however seems to have more clearly influenced by the Germanic model which divided them into *demands* for the return by the defendant of land or some other thing that properly belonged to the demandant and *complaints* that the defendant had done something wrong to the harm of the *plaintiff* (note the word). In either case the demandant (or complainant) appeared in court with their opponent and (with their hand on the property or some symbol of it) formally complained saying:

"Alan who is here complains of William who is there that (description of the property); the plaintiffs claim to it or allegation of the wrong done to him and the damage) and demands its return (seeks damages for it)."

In the case of a debt he would say:

"Alan who is here demands of William who is there that he restore to Alan the sum of forty marks which he received from him on midsummer day last past and was to have returned at Michelmas but has not done so though requested thrice."

In addition to this it was necessary that the plaintiff offer *proofs and suit,* for no one should suffer in either property or person on the mere say-so of another. These terms however had a rather peculiar meaning in those times (pre and immediately post conquest): suit, *secta* in Latin, meant that the plaintiff (or demandant) came supported by substantial persons who believed that his claim was well founded. They might or might not have knowledge about the matter but would not be questioned about that; it was enough that they supported the plaintiff's case. The offer of proof on the other hand might be to submit to an inquest, or to prove the rightness of the claim with his body or with the body of his freeman, Ralph (trial by battle) or by swearing an oath. This offer was followed by the phrase "or otherwise as the court shall appoint" for the decision of the court once the issue was joined in this way, was to state how proof should be made.

In response to the complaint (or demand) the defense might be that there was no need to reply as the complainant was an outlaw, a minor or some other person who had no right to appear in court, or perhaps that the court in question was not competent to hear the case. If nothing of this sort could be asserted then the defense would be the *general denial.* William would stand forth (perhaps laying his hand on the object in dispute) and deny Alan's claim in similar terms, an event which came to be described in the courts as defending word for word. He would likewise offer to defend his cause with his body or otherwise as the court shall appoint. The court would then decide on the mode of proof and he parties would give gage to carry out the behest of the court at the time and place appointed.

It would seem then that evidence and procedure as we have come to know it had no place in these traditional trials. The parties stood forth with claim and counterclaim, the court declared the form that proof should take and the issue was decided accordingly. However, the matter was not quite so simple. If any facts relevant to the case were well known or obvious, proofs would not be needed; a document under seal was, for instance, considered proof and in borough courts a cut stick (tally) was considered proof of a debt (or its repayment). Proof in the form of the ordeal or an oath would only be required if the decision rested on the word of the parties only. Moreover the entire procedure was in the nature of an ordeal. Each party had to get through the recitation of their case without mistakes and it may well have been feared that some blunder would inevitably take place if they were swearing falsely. The parties and those who stood with them as suitors had also to live with their neighbors after the case was over. It is hardly surprising then that a common result of such cases was that the parties sought leave to compromise, presumably when one or other of them got cold feet.

The customary forms of procedure were adopted initially by the royal courts, but some changes could normally be expected almost immediately and others would soon develop. To begin with, the fact that the proceedings were normally started off by the issuance of an original writ added one more hurdle to the obstacle race. The pleadings should not vary from those in the original writ or the case would fail. To avoid this, the parties would hire attorneys to plead for them. Indeed it is believed that one of the main reasons for this, at least initially, was that the attorney could make errors in pleading without implicating his principal.

The most important changes in the above procedural system were brought about by the development of the trial jury. In the late twelfth and early thirteenth century it was possible to purchase the privilege of an inquest of the country. This was a body of people from the neighborhood who could be expected to know something about the matter in dispute. We have seen how these juries were used to present criminals to the county court and to decide matters relating to seisin of land. They soon began to be used for demands and complaints generally. If the event complained of or the thing demanded was in a certain place, the juries from the four surrounding vills (North, South, East and West) would be empaneled and asked what they thought about it. The church in the early thirteenth century was skeptical about both ordeals and oaths. The ecclesiastical authorities, battling against a new crop of heresies, had found that many a hardy heretic was escaping from the church courts by means of the oath *(jurum canonici)* nor were they much impressed by the other ordeals. The same feeling seems to have been shared by the King's justiciars who did all that they could to have cases settled by means of the inquest. The inquest in England however was by the men of the countryside not by judicial inquisition as on the continent.

§7 *The science of pleading*

Pleading was never a simple matter, one had to get it just right, but it did not become complex enough to be interesting until courts began to consider pleas other than the general denial word by word. These alternative pleas were called *exceptions.* The first exceptional pleas were probably raised in connection with the possessory assizes (late thirteenth century). If William had recently moved into Greenacre where Alan had been seised, the petty jury in an action of *novel disseisin* would, considering the general question only, have to find for Alan. However, if Ranulf had granted to William a remainder in Grenacre contingent on the death of Matilda the wife of Alan, the plea would be an exception and would be entered by Williiam to stop the assize from proceeding any further (*quod non debet assiza inde fieri).* Exceptions were soon allowed in the other possessory assizes and thereafter in pleas of any type. Considering exceptions opened up many procedural questions and the business of pleading became, in the hands of the serjeants at law, a complicated formal system described by its practitioners as a science. The year books of the early fourteenth century show these masters of procedure fencing adroitly with one another under the supervision of the judge, (himself a former serjeant at law) and licking the plea into shape. Littleton writing to his son in the fifteenth century described it as the supreme science and it certainly operated under precise and strictly consistent rules. Each plea should be made only once (the rule against double pleading) and in its proper place in the proceedings. Pleading could not be argumentative and the plaintiff had to choose his action, i.e. he could not begin with a common law action and then change and seek an equitable remedy. There were some curious rules such as there could not be an affirmative pregnant with an negative (i.e. no innuendos). Many of these rules carried formalism too far but a number of them remain in the current rules of evidence, e.g the rule that a serjeant could not plead evidence.

Once the pleadings were established, the factual determinations would be decided by the jury. It was of course also possible that the facts could be accepted by both sides and settlement of the case sought on points of law only, e.g. whether a minor could bring the action in question or whether it was barred by the fact that the estate in question was not a freehold. This was called a demurrer from the Norman-French *demourir* which means to stop. All argument by counsel thereupon ceased and the case was decided on the pleadings before the court.

Originally one who pleaded an exception would have to offer suit and proof just as the original plaintiff (demandant) had done and could therefore be required to do battle or produce oath helpers. Since, however, the first exceptions were introduced in the context of the petty assizes, *recognitors* (representatives of the county) would normally be present and the questions raised by the exception could be put to them. The procedure of the jury trial and the science of pleading ultimately developed then side by side.

producing a body of custom which became the basis for the then contemporary courtroom practice.

§8. *The procedural significance of the record*

To start with, all pleading was oral and some latitude was allowed to the litigants until the pleadings were enrolled (entered on the plea roll). At that point the judge might warn the serjeants, as he did in one case, to be careful how the spoke from then on as what they say will be written. This is In contrast to the court records of the period in continental Europe (which gave a concise summary of the substance of the case). The English plea rolls recorded only formal matters, such as the original counts, the exceptions pleaded, the replies (replicts) of the first party etc. An important point was the recording of the final selection of the writ. In the early part of the thirteenth century the court clerks appear to have standardized the pleadings associated with each writ and these forms remained fairly constant for about six hundred years (till the nineteenth century when the forms of action were finally abolished).

The records were originally unavailable to the parties and the serjeants had no control over what the clerks might write. Bracton's book (mid thirteenth century.) made their contents public for the first time. Anything which was recorded could not be denied (it was the record of the King's justiciars) and appeals, in so far as they existed, were based on these records. Other courts might keep records but they were not courts of record. If an appeal was made from a local to a royal court, the writ of *recordari ad loquelam* was issued so that a special record of the local court's proceedings could be made anew under the supervision of the King's officer, the sheriff. Since the court records were of such importance it is not surprising that the serjeants at law wished to have more control over what was entered into them. They began therefore in the late thirteenth century. to present written pleadings to the clerks who would enter them into the roll.

Current court records are put together somewhat differently but many of these principles still apply in common law courts but not in European courts, which follow civil law.

§9 *Proceedings under a writ and proceedings by bill*

Proceedings by bill, where a simple statement of claim could be made and no original writ was necessary, derive from the right of any citizen to make a complaint to the King. As various courts spun off from the Royal curia, they tended to follow the formulary system (since the king was not present) where each case must be originated by a writ issued in chancery. Nevertheless the bill procedure remained as an alternative in some of these courts especially the King's Bench and the Court of Chancery, both of which theoretically retained a close connection with the curia regis. Proceedings by bill were less technical, speedier and above all, since they did not require the exorbitantly expensive services of a serjeant pleader, less costly than proceedings by original writ. They therefore became popular. A *bill of Middlesex* for instance could be used to bring a debtor into the King's Bench and collect the debt free from problems with essoins and warranty of oath which plagued the writ of debt/detinue. If someone happened to be before the king on some other business a private suitor would be allowed to bring an additional action against them at the same time e.g. for debt. This ancient privilege was made the basis of a legal fiction in the court of King's Bench, after that court had *ceased* to follow the king and become settled in London in the county of Middlesex. A creditor might be summoned there to answer a debt to the King and since this was a legal fiction the alleged debt was not traversable, i.e. it could not be denied. Once in court on this fictitious charge the defendant could be sued on some other matter by the plaintiff who had caused the Bill of Middlesex to be issued. If the defendant was not in fact available in Middlesex and refused to come there, a special writ (the writ of *latitat*) was issued to the Sheriff of Middlesex so that he could arrest the defendant wherever he might be and bring him into King's Bench to answer.

The records, as was mentioned earlier, were originally unavailable to the parties and the serjeants had no control over what the clerks might write. Bracton's book (mid thirteenth century) made their contents public for the first time. Anything which was recorded could not be denied (it was the record of the King's justiciars) and appeals, in so far as they existed, were based on these records. Other courts might keep records but they were not courts of record, their records were not necessarily accepted as proof of what had been done there. Witnesses would be required to testify under oath as to the proceedings in the lesser court.

Since the court records were of such importance it is not surprising that the serjeants at law wished to have more control over what was entered into them. They began therefore in the late thirteenth century to hand written pleadings to the clerks to have them entered into the roll.

Contemporary court records are put together somewhat differently but many of these principles still apply in common law courts but not in courts following the civil law tradition.

SPECIMEN PLEADINGS

Frenche v. Baker

Middlesex. John Baker, husbandman, was attached to answer Thomas Frenche concerning a plea of trespass by bill. And there are pledges for prosecuting, to wit, Richard Rous and Hugh Hunt. And thereupon the same Thomas, in his own person, complains that the aforesaid John on 17 Nov 1469 with force and arms, that is to say, with swords, staves and so forth - broke and entered the house of him the said Thomas at Westbourne in the aforesaid county, and then and there made assault upon him the said Thomas and beat, wounded and ill treated him and inflicted other outrages upon him, against the peace of the lord King aforesaid; whereby he says he is the worse and has damage to the value of twenty pounds. And thereof he produces suit. And the aforesaid John Baker by Thomas Luyt his attorney, comes and denies the force and wrong when [and where he ought] *[plea of guilty as to all but the assault]* And as to the coming with force and arms, or whatever is against the peace of the lord King, and all the aforesaid trespass except the assault aforesaid, he says that he is in no wise guilty thereof. And of this he puts himself upon the country. And the aforesaid Thomas French likewise.

And as to the assault, the same John Baker says that the aforesaid Thomas Frenche ought not to maintain his aforesaid action against him for that; because he says that the aforesaid Thomas Frenche on the aforesaid 17 November at Westbourne aforesaid, made assault upon him the said John and would then and there have beaten, wounded and ill treated him. And the same John then and there defended himself against the aforesaid Thomas. and if any ill then and there came to the same Thomas, it was a result of Thomas's own assault and in defence of him the said John. *[Averment]* And this he is ready to verify *[Conclusion si actio]* And so he prays judgement whether the aforesaid Thomas ought to maintain his aforesaid action against him therein.

[Replication de injuria] And the aforesaid Thomas says that he ought not to be barred by anything so far alleged from having his aforesaid action against him for the assault aforesaid. Because he says that the aforesaid John at the time when the aforesaid trespass was done, of his own wrong and without the cause alleged by him the said John above in his pleading, made assault upon the aforesaid Thomas Frenche with force and arms in the way that the same Thomas above complains against him. *[Joinder of issue]* And this he prays may be inquired into by the country. And the aforesaid John likewise.

Court of Broughton on Tuesday next after the feast of the Beheading of S John Baptist in the said year (1291).

The Earl of Oxford (distrained by three horses), the tenants of the land of Barnaby of Stukely (respited by the Abbot), William of Whiston and the tenants of the land of Berengar le Moyne have been elected to do the service due to the King according to the custom of the Abbey as appears above. And the said Earl does not come and has been three times distrained by three horses, as the rideman testifies. Therefore let them be detained and more be taken until etc. Let the tenants of the land of Barnaby of Stukely be distrained for the same. Let the tenants of the land of William of Whiston be distrained for the same. The Abbot holds the lands which sometime were Berengar's etc.

Brother Harry Damary, Commander of Keele, who complained of John Bird and Harry of Ashbourne of unjust detinue of sixty shillings, hath failed to prosecute his complaint against them. So this same Brother Harry and his pledges for prosecution are in mercy, to wit, John Lovett and Richard Partridge etc.

It was found by the Jury on which Harry of Ashbourne put himself at the suit of Brother Harry Damary, Preceptor of Keele, that the same Harry received thirty shillings from John Bird of the moneys which the aforesaid Brother Harry lost as he was passing through the town of Newcastle-under Lyme on St

Michael's Day last past. So judgement is given that the aforesaid Brother Harry recover the aforesaid thirty shillings against him. And the aforesaid Harry [of Ashbourne] is in mercy.

Edith that was wife of Richard of Darlaston complaineth to the Justices of our lord the King that whereas Richard her husband had taken at a rent from Amice that was wife of Harry of Verdun of Darlaston half a virgate of land, together with the houses, meadow and all appurtenances to the aforesaid land appertaining for [a fine] of seven marks and a half, paid in advance, to hold to the aforesaid Richard and Edith his wife and their heirs or assigns, for twenty years, rendering therefore to the aforesaid Amice one mark annually, the term beginning in the eighth year of the reign of King Edward, and whereas the aforesaid Richard and Edith continued for nine years in the aforesaid land, meadow and houses, in which same ninth year the aforesaid Richard died, and on the day that he died, while he yet lay dead within the aforesaid house, the aforesaid Amice came and ejected the aforesaid Edith and her six children from the aforesaid houses, land and everything, because Richard her husband was dead and she caused her barn to be sealed up and then caused all the corn that was then lying in that barn to be thrashed, to wit, twelve bushels of wheat, of the value of twelve shillings, [and] one quarter of hay, by weight, of the value of nine pence; and she caused this corn to be taken to her own house, **so** that the aforesaid Edith and her children have been able to have naught thereof; nor ever since up to now hath she had entry on the aforesaid land, messuage or meadow, to her grievous damage of marks and more; of which she prayeth you remedy of your charity for God's sake for she is poor, and by these things she has been brought to beggary.

Furthermore this same Edith has made and delivered to the sheriff a bill in respect of these things and is cheated of it, and she knoweth not how, save it be because the aforesaid Amice is rich and is the sister of Sir Roger of Penlesdown; wherefore she prayeth you that you will take pity on her, and that she may have judgement of this bill and be not cheated of it as of the one before.

CHAPTER FIVE
THE REVIEW PROCESS

§1 The several competing courts and resulting confusion

During the twelfth century the King's system of justice began to be established independently of and separate from the customary courts which had existed before the Norman conquest. So the various eyres which had been devised to supervise the administration of criminal law and other pleas of the Crown began to hear common pleas, and the Court of Common Pleas was established in London. The nisi prius system, established in the fourteenth century, allowed the legal aspects of a case (licking the plea into shape) to be carried out at Westminster Hall in London while the determination of matters of fact could be made by a local jury in the county where the case originated. This relieved the jurymen of the impossible burden of travelling to London on every case. The Nisi Prius system greatly extended the amount of work that could be done by the five Justices of Common Pleas in London. In the fourteenth and fifteenth century other courts began to compete with the court of Common Pleas for business. The court of King's Bench, the Court of the Exchequer and the Court of Chancery were already in existence, each with its own proper sphere of business: but law was profitable and they were soon to hear virtually any case which might come under the aegis of the common law. In addition to the common law courts, there were also the various communal courts such as county courts, manorial courts (courts baron and courts leet) and of course the ecclesiastical courts. All of these institutions competed with one other very actively during the middle ages.

The Court of Exchequer used legal fictions of one sort or another to pretend that a suit somehow involved the King's interests and was particularly interested in cases of debt. The court of King's Bench used the fiction of the Bill of Middlesex to hale suitors into court on a pretended charge. Once they were present the court exercised the

right to hear any other matter which might be brought against them by a private person.

How did such a variety of courts affect the administration of justice. To some extent it encouraged innovation and improvement as each sought to attract suitors away from the other or to protect their turf. So a remedy originally developed in King's bench (e.g. some variety of trespass action) was likely to be adopted by Common Pleas. Similarly forms and remedies developed originally in Chancery or in the ecclesiastical courts were imported into the procedure of the common law courts.

§2. *Removing a case from one court to another*

In addition to offering one another free competition,

courts developed special writs which could be used to remove a case from another court. If it was removed before judgement was handed down it was termed a *transfer;* if the case had already been decided in the other court it was called an *appeal.* These are still the terms used to describe such transactions and they are defined in much the same way. If it is concluded that a court is not competent to hear a case it will be transferred whereas complaints that it was wrongly decided with give rise to an appeal.

§3 The true appellate writs - recordari and certiorari

The writs of *pone* and *tolt* were ancient remedies which were developed by the royal justices to remove cases concerning land from feudal into royal courts. By the writ of tolt *a* case could be removed from a seignorial court into the county court and from there it could be transferred to Common Pleas by the writ of pone. Pone and tolt were used along with the writ of right to ensure that all cases concerning title to a freehold not only could be but eventually were heard before the Royal Justices.

Another ancient writ, that of recordari *(recordari facias loquelam* ("let what was said be recorded"), existed as a last appeal from a feudal court to that of the King. This is an appeal not a transfer and what was done in the manorial court was evidenced not by a written record (even if one existed) but by the testimony of four knights. Such appeals could be decided in the royal court or (as in Hamo's case) returned to the local court to be decided in accordance with the instructions of the royal judge.

The writ of *certiorari* was originally a royal request for information. Thus a sheriff of a township might be asked to return data to the royal court. Very quickly it became used as a method of appeal. In 1271 an assize of *darrein presentment* was removed from the commission which usually heard such cases locally, to the court of common pleas because of undue delay. In this *case* the cause was mentioned but later the writ simply stated that the King wishes to know what is going on to be sure of a cause. Very early (from about 1280) it was used as a form of the *writ of error.* The losing party could apply for it. Certiorari was used for a time by the chancellors to review the proceedings of the common law courts but this practice quickly died out and the chancellors merely reviewed the work of their own assistants and inferiors with this writ. It was used to review hearings of special boards such as the work of the commissioners of assize. It was used also to spring documents and information from officials who were refusing to hand over the documents or provide information. It could also be employed by the Court of Chancery to bring cases before it for execution, or where it was suspected that records submitted (e.g. on appeal) were incomplete (diminished). The writ continued to be used for this purpose into modern times. In the form described by Fitzherbert it has at its close the phrase that "having inspected the record--- we may cause further to be done thereupon." In the United States this writ was used to initiate an appeal not to obtain information.

§4 *The writ of false judgement (de falso judicio)*

In customary courts the decision was given by all those attending the proceedings, called doomsmen since it was their task to render a decision (doom). Challenging the decision of the doomsmen was in effect giving them the lie (since their decision was based their own knowledge) and calling anyone a liar was of course an open challenge to instant battle with axes. To replace such unseemly proceedings with the King's peace the writ *de falso iudicio* was introduced. This commanded the sheriff that "recordari facias loquelam" should be taken and four suitors, either orally or with a written summary, went to the King's court. If a disappointed suitor was successful here, the local court might be fined. Hamo's case previously mentioned was just such a case. However, the Court of the Earl of Brittany was not fined, the matter was simply remanded back there for reconsideration.

§5 *The writ of error*

The writ of error is different from both the certiorari and the writ of false judgement. It was obviously in existence prior to 1285 since it had to be amended in that year by the Statute of Westminster II. It appears to have been a royal writ and was aimed at error in the record. Consequently when this writ was issued from Chancery to a common law court, the court record or a certified copy of it had to be sealed and returned along with the writ. Thus it was very like a certiorari, but since it stayed all further proceedings e.g. an entered judgement had to be stayed, it acted like a *supersedias*. It was not however merely a review of the record since both parties could be summoned to take part in the proceedings. It could be issued in criminal as well as civil cases. In serious cases e.g. where someone had been convicted of a serious crime, the losing party was not entitled to the writ as a matter of right, it might or might not be issued. In less serious matters it was issued as a matter of course (*de cursu*) although the court might refuse to hear the case. But even in serious cases it was unusual to refuse the writ if the claim that an error had occurred had any substance to it.

The writ of error had serious defects. The main difficulty was that evidence which was refused by the lower court would not be in the record and so could not be reviewed. Chapter 31 of the Statute of Westminster II (1285 a.d.) therefore required that when an exception (an alternative plea to the general denial) was requested and refused, the plea sought and its refusal should be entered into the record so that the matter could be reviewed on proceedings in error. Questions of fact, even when decided by a jury and duly evidenced in the record, have nevertheless remained difficult on appeal. If there is nothing technically wrong, e.g. that the jury were wrongly instructed as to the law, a jury finding has to be completely perverse before it can be reversed. Originally a judge acting on the authority of the royal prerogative. could review a jury decision and even punish jurors for what was considered a wrong decision. But this kind of review perished and only erroneous giving or withholding of evidence from the jury or some other technical fault can be used to reverse a jury decision.

§6   Review of jury decisions

Queen Elizabeth tried jurors who had decided a case against the crown and caused them to be paraded around Westminster with placards on their back proclaiming their folly. This was perceived to be oppressive and after Chief Justice Vaughan's decision in Bushnell's case, the only way to proceed against a jury decision (other than on a procedural question) was by the action of *attaint*. Actions of attaint were not uncommon throughout the thirteenth century and there is evidence that juries were concerned about the possibility of being tried in such an action. Some even believe that it was the voicing of such concerns that allowed the jury to bring in special verdicts and throw the responsibility of the final determination of the case back on the judge. The penalties invoked against the jury were, however, severe and since such cases were tried before another jury it is understandable that the latter were not inclined to find the earlier jury guilty very often. Consequently the action of attaint declined very rapidly in popularity from the fourteenth century on and had almost, if not altogether, disappeared in the Elizabethan era. Only procedural questions then could be reviewed using the action of error. A jury verdict might then be reversed by claiming that a jury question had not been raised by the evidence, that the jury were misdirected or that requested testimony was not allowed into evidence or testimony allowed which should have been refused. Later new evidence was allowed as a ground for a second jury trial on criminal charges.

$7 *Appellate courts*

As the various courts became established and competed with one another for business, the review prerogative of King's *bench* was *used* against the other courts. In the fourteenth century King's bench sought to review questions from the court of Exchequer, a maneuver strongly resisted by the latter court. When this controversy was at its height in 1358 the court of *Exchequer Chamber* was set up to amend errors in the exchequer. This court consisted of the chancellor and treasurer of the exchequer and such other common law judges as they should call in to assist them. This process in Exchequer Chamber came to be used by all the royal courts. It was not however an appeal such as might be brought by a writ in error. It was rather initiated by the judges themselves when a difficult question was raised and the trial judge deemed that a consultation was advisable. It was invoked e.g. in *Calvin's case* when the right of a Scotsman to English justice was discussed. Cases with a constitutional aspect or where the law was being altered or radically interpreted, might also be suitable for hearing in Exchequer Chamber. In Tudor and Stuart times the royal prerogative courts, such as Star Chamber, began to hear appeals from common law courts but following the restoration in 1688 the prerogative courts and the court of Exchequer Chamber both disappeared. Only the House of Lords remained as the ultimate court of appeal. Until 1850 all the peers of the realm, lay and judicial, gave judgement, just as a manorial court would have done in the middle ages. Lay lords were excluded from legal appeals in 1850 (by Lord Campbell) but the medieval origins of this court are still manifest e.g. by the fact that a peer of the realm can still insist on being tried for a serious crime by his peers, in the House of Lords (a procedure more or less obsolete).

§8 *The writ of prohibition*

This was originally a royal command to a court to desist. It came however to be a writ that any citizen could apply for, in Common Pleas or King's Bench, requesting that some inferior or regional court, such as a court of the marches (borders) or an ecclesiastical court, should be commanded to desist in a case either because the matter was out of their jurisdiction or because the manner in which they were conducting it was contrary to the common law. The ecclesiastical courts e.g., were at one time commanded on a writ of prohibition to require two witnesses to the payment of a legacy in order to bring their practice into line with the Statute of Wills.

An appeal to Chancery could be made if the common law courts refused to issue a prohibition. It was necessary in this case to show that there was otherwise no remedy as "equity follows the law". Sir Edward Coke used prohibitions

during the struggle with the Stuart monarchy to virtually strangle the ecclesiastical courts.

§9 *The writ of mandamus.*

Unlike the writ of prohibition, a command to desist, mandamus was a command to a person or an institution to act and do their duty. Direct royal commands of this nature were issued in early times but mandamus was not seen as a regular formal writ until 1573 when it was issued to restore to a London merchant a franchise of which he had been deprived. One of the famous cases was *Bagg's case,* reported by Coke in 1615. Here a pro forma writ of mandamus was issued by King's bench requiring the mayor and commonalty of Plymouth to restore Bagg to his office. The use of this writ is always related to public or quasi-public matters e.g. admissions of duly elected officials to their office if they have been prevented or hindered in any way.

§10 *Quo warranto*

This writ requires any official who has done, or wishes to do something, to show by what right he does so. It is an old remedy, preceding the statutes of *quo warranto* of Edward I in 1284. Its nature is that of a writ of right issued on behalf of the King. It was commonly used to challenge a franchise. If the franchise is disallowed it may either fall into complete disuse or be regranted by the king to someone else. The judgement associated with it, to dispossess the franchise holder, was called an *ouster.* If the franchise were upheld there was no appeal by the Crown since the matter was already being directly determined between the subject and the Crown. Being a writ of right it was subject to *essoins* etc. which could lead to unconscionable delays. A more modem procedure had to be developed which worked by *informations* which were filed by the attorney general. This was not only speedier but appeal was possible. This procedure also carried with it penalties for misuse of the franchise. In civil cases these penalties were frequently nominal, unlike criminal informations elsewhere. In this form, as an information lodged with the attorney general at the instigation of a private person, *quo warranto* became a popular way of proceeding against officials in the eighteenth century. Note that it affects both the right to use a franchise and its wrongful use.

§11 *Ne exeat regno*

This writ relates to the privilege of the crown to refuse the common law right of a citizen (mentioned by Magna Carta) to go abroad. Fitzherbert relates it to the requirement that the King is entitled to help in defense of the realm. Other rationales have been suggested. Coke thought it was related to the movements of clergy and was used as a means of controlling ecclesiastical appeals out of the country to Rome. It was issuable by the prayer of any of the principal secretaries of state and there was no need to show cause. It could also be used to bring someone back into the realm on pain of forfeiture.

§12 *The writ of habeas corpus*

We have seen that the writ of certiorari was used as a means of removing causes from administrative or statutory courts. The writ of habeas corpus was often associated with it to remove the defendant from these courts also. Together they were sometimes abused as means of evading liability in lower courts. Likewise they were used by officials of higher courts to deprive defendants in lower courts of justice there and to bring them into their own hands. The writ of habeas corpus was used in many ways to compel a litigant in a lower court to answer in a higher one. Many words were associated with it depending on the use intended for it. It would be described as *habeas corpus ad respondam* when someone was imprisoned by order of an inferior court and it was wished to have them appear and answer to a greater charge. *Habeas corpus ad satisfaciendum* was the expression used when it was wished to execute a judgement in a court higher than the one in which it had been obtained. When the action of a lower court was being questioned and it was deemed necessary to produce the person as well as the information about the circumstances and cause of the arrest, then the writ was called *habeas corpus cum causa.*

It has already been mentioned that habeas corpus together with certiorari could be used to avoid judgments and to cause delays. Various rules were devised to prevent these abuses. Small suits of less than five pounds value could not be removed from a lower court at all and those under ten pounds could not be moved without surety for the amount. Likewise habeas corpus could not apply after issue was joined in a court provided the court was presided over by a competent judge. The writ of *habeas corpus ad subjiciendum* was the form used by Coke and others as a defense against illegal arrest and confinement. It orders that the prisoner shall be produced before the judge issuing the writ, to submit to and receive whatever the court shall consider and award on his behalf. It was only issued out of King's Bench and was considered so important that it could be issued at any time of the year, not only during term time. One must apply for it to the court in session because it was a prerogative writ and could not be obtained as of right. This was to prevent it from being used frivolously. Coke indeed denied a habeas corpus to a notorious pirate who was in prison. The writ required showing of no probable cause.

§13 *De non procedendo rege inconsulto*[1]

This writ was used in the 13th century to remove a case from lower courts into chancery or exchequer or some other court where the king's interest might be better safeguarded. It was considered to lie in cases where there was a crown interest in the proceedings. It was the subject of a good deal of controversy in the constitutional struggles of the 17th century and though never really abolished, it became obsolete. Any remaining functions that it might have had were carried out by an injunction rather than a non procedendo.

§14 *The appellate court system*

In the twelfth century it was possible to appeal a decision of the King's justices (on eyre or in common pleas) to the court of the king himself and such appeals were soon

---

[1] I.e. not to proceed without consulting the King.

delegated to a special group of justiciars known as the King's bench (*coram regis*). A case might not indeed be appealed directly to the King without having previously been heard in King's bench. The writ *coram vobis* was used to appeal a case from Common Pleas to King's Bench. If the case had been heard in King's Bench and was being appealed to the King's council the appropriate writ was *coram nobis.* This ultimate appeal to the presence of the King came eventually to be exercised by the House of Lords which was indeed the feudal court of the king.

A true appellate system of courts was set up in England by the Judicature Act of 1875 establishing the Court of Appeals as an intermediate appellate court with final appeal to the House of Lords. However, cases being appealed from commonwealth countries outside England, such as Australia, were not appealed to the House of Lords, an English feudal court, but directly to the Crown. This review was in fact exercised by a group of advisors to the Crown known as the *Privy Council.* Since the Privy council delegated these hearings to law lords, in actual fact they were heard by much the same people who heard cases arising on appeal in England.

CHAPTER SIX
PROPERTY

§1   *Feudalism*

The term "feudal" was popularized by Blackstone in the first edition of his Commentaries (1766). The word was known previously, but Blackstone's predecessor Coke made little use of it. Blackstone derived his understanding of the term from works on legal history by Sir Martin Wright and Sir Henry Spellman and it has been suggested that he unnecessarily complicated the law of real property by introducing that term into it. Be this as it may, the term and the concepts associated with it have become part of the law of property and here as elsewhere an authoritative misinterpretation becomes the law.

The term feudal comes from the Latin *feodum* (an oath). Its essence being that land is not held directly by the owner but as the result of a personal relationship between two people, the lord and the tenant. The tenant pays (and the lord receives) *homage.* The tenant is then bound to perform certain *services,* depending on the nature of the tenure. The feudal lord likewise has obligations, notably to *warrant* the title of the tenant to the land in question. Mutual help and protection was however, at least in the beginning, implied. The tenant might for instance be obligated to help ransom his lord should he be captured during battle, to contribute to the knighting of his eldest son and to help supply a dowry for his oldest daughter, these various forms of help due to the lord were lumped together under the term *aids.* The direct services were called *rents.* There were also certain rights (originally duties) of the lord called *incidents.* The lord had to protect the estate of the tenant should he die prematurely, look after his widow, bring up and educate his sons particularly the heir to his *estate* (*wardship*) and arrange suitable marriages for his daughters (*marriage*). In order to do this the lord took over the estate although he had to account for it to the heir when he came of age. The incidents of wardship and marriage were in fact very lucrative to the feudal lord and Henry VIII as the ultimate feudal lord had to set up a special court to look after his interest in his wards.

§2   *The origins of feudalism*

The origin of feudalism is generally traced to the 9th century a.d. At that time it was developed as a method of organization made necessary by the invasions of the Norsemen and the general breakdown of society. However, similar arrangements had already been in existence before the Norse invasions. The system of taxation imposed in the later Roman empire and the barbarian kingdoms which followed it, made things so difficult for small landholders that they were forced to cede all their rights unconditionally to more powerful persons or to religious corporations in return for protection. They remained on the land and shared the profits but the relationship was called *precarious tenure* (*precor* means I pray and they could only pray to be allowed to remain on the lands at the goodwill of their patron). This system survived long in Italy as *patronage.* The ecclesiastical version was known as benefice since those who remained on the land did so only as the result of the good will of their ecclesiastical protectors. An ecclesiastical appointment to a church thus became known as benefice and usually implied a holding in land.

§3 *The Norman version of military feudalism*

The feudal system applied by William the Conqueror in England, made military tenure the most important form of service. Each tenant had to supply so many knights or foot soldiers or archers or whatever, as a condition of his tenure. William I also arranged that the *feodum* or oath should be held directly of him, not indirectly through the immediate feudal lord. Yet even in military tenure there were other obligations. The tenant was expected to attend and give advice as a suitor (from *suivre-* to follow) at the lord's court and the lord conversely was expected to see that his tenants got justice. The legal aspects of the court of the King originated in this manner and the court of King's Bench derived from the immediate tenants of the king meeting as his counsel and also to decide disputes among themselves of a legal nature. The legal duty of *suit was* considered very burdensome and important persons sought the privilege of being represented at customary courts by one of their tenants. In course of time only unimportant persons were present as suitors in such courts and this contributed to their decline.

§4 *The difference between tenure and ownership*

In Roman law the owner of property had *dominium,* complete ownership which carried the rights to use (*utere*) to abuse (*abutere*) to enjoy (*fruere*) and to destroy (*destruere*). Original feudal tenants did not have such an extensive estate in land. They did not own the property, they held it of a feudal lord and as such their estate was called a holding or (in Norman French) a *tenement.* True dominium in this system lay only in the King and if the estate of the tenant failed for any reason the estate reverted to the immediate lord and ultimately to the King. The Latinized German word for dominium was *allodium,* an allode being a parcel of land which is owned by someone absolutely. Blackstone therefore refers to land which is held in true ownership as *allodial* land.

§5   *The terms freehold and fee*

The derived interest in land held by a tenant could be of several types and the form of the holding (fee simple, tenure for life etc.) came to be known as the *estate* in land. The importance of a person was measured by their land holdings and so could also be termed their estate (the term status comes from it). If the tenant had a right to stay there till he died it was called a *freehold estate.* When the heir of a deceased tenant entered into the estate (increasingly he was allowed and indeed had the right to do so) this was done by the heir paying homage i.e. taking the oath (feodom) of fealty. The heritable aspects of the estate, i.e. the tenants right to pass on the tenement to their heirs and assigns, became known as the *fee.* By the end of the 12th century the fee no longer meant a personal oath (feodum) made to the lord but rather a holding in land. It indicated the fact that the estate in land, whatever it was, belonged to the tenant and was their property, it was not merely an interest held at will of their feudal lord. The lord also had a right in this land which was known as the *seignory* (lordship). Whoever had the fee paid the rents and (more importantly) the incidents took their rise from the holder of the fee. The idea of a divided fee was therefore repugnant to medieval lawyers who were wont to ask when considering a complex settlement or grant "where is the fee? or sometimes "who will pay homage?". The rule in Shelley's case and other doctrines (incomprehensible to modern eyes) were developed to avoid this difficulty.

§6 *The feudal incidents*

The original rents and services rendered under military tenure were totally unsuitable for maintaining a standing army, especially foreign service in France, and they were commuted to money payments called *scutage* or shield money. The devaluation of money made these payments of very little worth and certain other aspects of the feudal relationship, especially the incidents, came to constitute the real value of a seignory to the feudal lord. The following are some of the more important examples:

1. Relief. Originally the death of the tenant ended the tenure and the estate could theoretically be awarded to anyone else that the lord chose. Quickly however the right of the heir to pay homage and be enfeoffed was recognized. The lord might however exact a payment for this privilege and this was known as a relief. Relief was much resented and eventually only remained between the king and his immediate tenants, the lords of the realm.

2. Wardship. The death of a tenant leaving an infant son enabled the lord to take all the profits until the son came of age. This was not like a Roman tutelage where the tutor had to account for all the profits and what was done for them and only had them in trust for the ward. In wardship the property was the lord's (except that he could not convey it away). He was only obliged to spend whatever was necessary for the proper education of the heir to fill his station in life. It was argued by those who favored this system, particularly in France, that the lord was the proper guardian of the infant's rights; that his mother might marry again, have another family etc., in whose interest the rights of the heir might be in jeopardy etc. The feudal lord on the other hand had no interest in taking the infant's life, and so was the proper guardian. Be this as it may, wardship was regarded as a great hardship by the tenants and much ingenuity was exercised in conveyancing to *uses etc.* to defeat this and other incidents.

3 .Marriage. It was felt that the lord had an interest in the marriage of his tenant's sons and daughters, as marriage might bring into the system someone who was his enemy or otherwise incompetent. The king in 1100 a.d. required his barons to consult him about the marriage of their daughters although this involved no payment to him. If a baron had died, the king might marry off his daughters and dispose of their lands to their husband. The same rule was stated under Henry II. In the writings of Glanville in 1193 we find the king selling the marriage of male heirs; it is no longer a matter of protecting the lord's interests, it has become a financial perquisite. The right of a lord to marry off the minor males and the daughters of a deceased tenant, together with wardship, came to be considered as the property of the lord and were indeed known as *chattels real.*

4. Escheat and forfeiture. If the tenant died without issue, the estate escheated to his lord, who was thus described by Bracton as "the ultimate heir". The tenant, faced with lack of issue, was not allowed to appoint an heir, the appropriate rule being that only God can make an heir (quite different from our modem notion and that of Roman law). If the tenant committed a felony the land escheated to his immediate lord, but the Crown was allowed to *waste* it for a year and a day. If the tenant was found guilty of treason the land *forfeited* directly to the crown. Escheats were sometimes created by feudal lords who had their tenants found guilty of fabricated felonies (such as theft of a cow) in order to take their land. Forfeiture for treason was considered a harsh penalty during the wars of the roses when everyone and their lord had to take sides and the losers were inevitably found guilty of treason. Pardons then became frequent and forfeitures avoided.

§7   *Various forms of tenure*

1. Military tenure. Knight service was the most important of these in the tenth century when the medieval knight, a light armored horsemen, was the key unit in battle. As the knights became important personages they tended to be protected by heavy and expensive armor so that the cost of maintaining knights became prohibitive. It therefore became he custom for the lord to accept a sum, somewhat less than the money required to equip a knight, and eventually a substitute payment called scutage or shield money was accepted in lieu of actual service. Knights became more or less obsolete after the Battle of Crecy where the English archers, equipped with the long bow, destroyed the flower of France's knights in a very short space of time. Knight service however persisted as a distinct form of tenure (mostly an honorific title). It was abolished by statute in 1660 and made equivalent to *socage* tenure (see below). A *serjeant* (Latin serviens) was originally the squire of the knight and serjeanty, grand and petty was a further form of military tenure which, like knight service, was abolished in 1660. Professional attorneys in the royal courts were often retained by great estates and religious houses by grants of land in serjeanty, and thus were known as serjeants at law.

2. Socage. The original meaning of the term soc is unclear. Grants to a major land holder for instance could be made with "soc and sac". Socage tenure however was a term applied to tenure where the services required were not of a military nature. Some tenants undertook to labor for so many days of the month in the fields of the lord or other tasks to be performed might be specified. By 1660 however socage tenure was considered to be like free ownership of the land and the military tenures were then converted by statute into "free and common socage". The guardian in wardship in socage was not the lord but a relative who was accountable to the heir like the Roman tutor. He could sell the heir's marriage but must account for the price to the heir. Some attempts were made by feudal lords to assert wardship over socage tenants but they failed.

3. *Burgage.* This was peculiar to towns, but did not apply in those that were so small as to be considered a vill. The laws and usages in towns tended to develop along their own lines and they long retained their own courts and customs. This was probably because they were centers of business and commerce and so could rightly claim to be totally different from the surrounding countryside. Many of the early colonists who settled in America were burghers and it is likely that the largely non- feudal nature of property law (including the law of succession) in America can be traced to this fact. Burgage tenure did not require homage and so was not subject to aids, marriage etc. although property could escheat or forfeit to the crown or perhaps to the borough in the event of felony or treason. Peculiar local customs often persisted in these boroughs and thus the ancient lien law customs of the Anglo-Saxons (where in order to alienate, the relatives had to be consulted) could be found in certain boroughs.

4. *Frankalmoign.* Frank means free and almoign means mercy (from the Greek *eleemos* merciful). Frankalmoign was tenure where the land had been given to the church in return for prayers. No feudal services or incidents were involved. This kind of gift however created a problem in feudal society since it took land out of the general political system. It was thus converted in France into some kind of feudal service so that an abbey or other spiritual corporation might be obliged to supply so many knights etc. to the king.

5. *Villeinage.* This originated in the vill or village which was originally a community of people running a largely agricultural enterprise. The mark theory, developed in 19th

century Germany, suggested that it involved a kind of communism. This was later shown to be incorrect and that the vill rather represents a collection of family enterprises with well defined individual rights and community rights of the contributing groups. As the royal justice established itself, the vills became heavily burdened with duties such *as* criminal presentments, court appearance, and jury service and the villeins in fact became such a depressed class that they were virtually slaves and serfs could not leave the vill. They rebelled ineffectively during the reign of Richard II but the effort was clearly unnecessary for events were already moving in directions which would lead to improvement in their conditions. The black death in particular made serfs so scarce that neighboring landlords competed for their services in order to be able to farm their estates. Justices of the peace were then charged with the duty of seeing that unfair competition did not result. The estates of the villeins were enrolled in a book and they had a copy of the entry so that they were known *as copyholders.* Their remedies were very good and in 1660 copyhold was recognized *as* being a freehold in land. People who held land in fee simple, indeed, sought to have their holding effectively changed to copyhold.

6. Dower. This was the right of married women to some share in the estate after the death of their husband. It was developed first by the ecclesiastical courts but also by the common law courts who were more determined even than the church courts to encourage marriage. Thus dower required a proper marriage and only applied to property that was owned "at the church door". Later it came to apply to property acquired at a later date. The amount of dower varied with the nature of the tenement. In socage tenure it was usually a third, in villeinage it was all of the property for life in some cases and half in others. It did not apply to joint tenancy nor to uses and this fact became important in the law of trusts.

7. Curtesy. William I did not take as conqueror but rather claiming to be the lawful king. The Normans therefore did not automatically dispossess all English theigns, only the disloyal ones, and so there was a considerable group of landed Anglo-Saxons who retained their property. Norman adventurers tended to marry propertied women and the law of curtesy is said to have been developed so that if these women died then the landless adventurers would at least be provided for during their lifetime. Curtesy only applied if a child had been born and the rule that the cry had to be heard within the four walls was commonly applied. Sometimes the child had to be seen, heard and baptized.

8. *Life estates.* Originally all feudal estates were for life only but as the fee became heritable, a true life estate became rare except in dower and curtesy or in the case of the tenant for life in fee tail. One of the problems created by the life estate was the question of waste i.e. cutting and selling trees or in some other way diminishing the value of the property for the remainderman. It was not felt that the full Roman Law action of account was applicable and so the action of waste only applied in cases of wanton destruction or gross negligence. A further question related to whether the petty assizes would lie for a dispossessed life tenant and it was felt eventually that they should e.g. the life tenant in fee tail should be able to recover from an ouster (since life tenants have a freehold estate).

10. Term of years. Most restrictive rules were originally applied to the lease for years and it was not considered a freehold estate. This was because it was not originally really an estate in land at all but really only a disguised form of a loan with interest at an extortionate rate which was contrary to law. The value of the term of years would greatly exceed the amount of money advanced and be in effect interest. Gradually however it was felt that it ought to be protected by law and Sir William Raleigh devised a writ for the dispossessed termor called *quare ejecit infra terminum* (since the defendant ejected the plaintiff before the term of years was finished). This and the writ *de ejectione firmae* (concerning ejection from ones farm) proved to be rather slow and unsatisfactory and the term of years did not come into its own until after the black death when villeins became suddenly valuable and were often able to acquire long leases in return for their services. Good remedies for the termor of years then became available. These were variants of the writ of trespass and were so effective that tenants who held in socage or in some other form of tenure, sought the same remedies by means of legal fictions involving leases for a term of years. These long leases of the villeins were then converted into copyhold and in 1660 into socage tenure.

§8 *Some legal problems relating to feudal theory*

During the first hundred years after the Norman conquest a number of troublesome questions were raised about feudal estates.

1. The question of *inheritance*. It was usual for the first son to be admitted to the estate on the death of his father. Sometimes the father would ask the feudal lord to take the homage of his heir before his death to protect this interest. Eventually however the claim of the heir to become seised came to be regarded as a legal right. The Norman rule of inheritance was though the eldest son (primogeniture) but this ran counter to native practices which tended in most cases to divide land between all the dependents. In one area, Kent, the practice of the Jute tribes from Denmark in giving the land to the youngest son and to divide all other property equally was allowed to remain. This custom was known as *gavelkind*. Local custom was, however, largely obliterated in the interests of the feudal system. By the time that Glanville wrote (late 12th century) primogeniture was the rule for knight service and the higher feudal estates, but local rules persisted in the boroughs and many of these were brought over by the earlier settlers to the American colonies.

94

2. *The question of the alienability of land.* In Anglo-Saxon times the consent of the family was required before land could be alienated even when the gift was to the church. In Glanville's time the question was still moot as to whether even a reasonable amount of land (in France one third) could be alienated. Deathbed gifts of land were clearly illegal and invalid in Glanville's time as it was felt that these might be foolish and prejudice the interests of the heirs and other parties. In the year 1200 the Fitz Nigel case illustrates the problems which could arise even though the gifts here were to members of the family not to strangers for value. In this case a parent deeded land to a younger son who had offered homage to the oldest son. This acceptance of homage was regarded as a sort of subinfeudation so that the older son accepted and acquiesced in the gift to the younger. One can see from this that it was still considered necessary to have the consent of the heir in order to make a gift to a younger son. It was also at this time necessary to have the consent of the heir in order to make a gift to the church.

3. The question of *subinfeudation.* The feudal system had been modified by major landholders dividing up their land and taking homage from lesser tenants i.e. by subinfeudation. The practice was still allowable in the time of Glanville but one case, decided in 1203 shows that there was considerable dissatisfaction with it. There were a number of parties likely to suffer as the result of the practice but the objections chiefly came from the feudal overlords. The feudal lord might find the tenant substituting someone who was unsatisfactory from the lord's point of view, perhaps even one of his enemies. Worse, he might find that the services associated with the gift were minimal, such as the gift of a rose at midsummer, and that the remaining lands were not sufficient to enforce the services of the original tenant by means of distraint. Worst of all, the feudal incidents would be diminished in value.

Various measures were taken from time to time to regulate this situation. In the third issuing of Magna Carta in 1217 there was a statement that no sale or alienation of feudal land could take place which was such that the residue would not support the feudal services. In 1290 the Statute known as *Quia emptores* prohibited subinfeudation and stated that if there was partition of land the feudal services must go with the land. This provision however only applied to the fee simple and was held not to apply to conditional or life estates. Some felt that *quia emptores* was a diabolical piece of royal legislation but this was probably not the case. It was indeed promulgated in the interests of the barons to ensure that they would receive their due feudal services. Its effect however was that, since further infeudation was prevented or at least discouraged, it allowed the normal course of forfeiture etc. to reduce the number of feudal estates still in existence and indeed tended to accumulate land in the upper echelons of the feudal hierarchy and so eventually into the hands of the king.

A more serious problem with alienation concerned gifts to ecclesiastical foundations. Since these were not real persons they could hardly commit felonies and since they never died they could not run short of an heir nor give rise to wardships and marriages. These last were most important as the feudal incidents eventually became the only profitable part of the feudal arrangement so far as lords were concerned (the rents having become hopelessly devalued). A great deal of revenue needed by the Crown to run the country was thus lost to the Church. Such a gift to the Church was described as *a mortmain* (dead hand). The Statute of Mortmain 1290 required authorization by the crown for such gifts and penalized unauthorized gifts by forfeiture to the lord in question. Extensive gifts were however in fact authorized to ecclesiastical foundations by the crown.

With so many loopholes in them, the rules against alienation were clearly inoperable and by the end of the thirteenth century it appears that land was freely alienable. The attention of conveyancers was now being directed to restricting the ability of landholders to convey land away to the detriment of their heirs.

§9 Conditional estates

The attempt to limit the alienation of land in a family by conditional gifts did not begin immediately after the conquest. However, there was in Anglo-Saxon times, *book land* (boc-land) where written title could be given in such a form as to limit the estates of several parties. This was at first limited to ecclesiastical estates but later was extended to others. Many of these operated very much like an entail.

Another development, within the feudal system, was the *maritagium.* This was, in effect, a marriage endowment with well known provisions. If the couple to be married did not have a child, the gift reverted to the grantor and in some cases was not handed over by him until the cry of the newborn child had been heard within the four walls. If the child subsequently died the grant remained in force so that there was some room here for fraud. In *the maritagiium t*he feudal incidents were suspended for four generations i.e. till the third heir came of age. He would then pay homage. This suspension of the feudal incidents allowed the family to become established without reliefs, wardships etc.. By Bracton's time (writing circa 1258) other more detailed gifts were being drafted to meet the needs of grantors who wished to provide for the continued existence of their family estate.

§10 Words of limitation and words of purchase

The earliest attempt to create an entailed estate by making a grant "to A and his heirs" was quickly interpreted as giving a fee simple to A. "To A for life and then to the heirs of his body" was given a similar interpretation i.e. on the birth of a child the estate became a fee simple. These expressions were taken as words of *limitation* and not *words of purchase* i.e. they showed the extent of the estate, that it was not simply a life estate, but did not make the heirs purchasers, i.e. persons who entered in their own right after the death of the present tenant. "To A and B and then to the heirs of their body" was similarly interpreted as a *conditional fee simple, where* the grant was being conditioned on them producing a life child as heir.

All this was contrary to the wishes and intentions of the grantors who included major magnates of the land and in 1258, during the barons revolt against Henry III, they petitioned the king that this state of affairs be altered. Edward I, then prince of Wales, was already interested in affairs of state especially legal matters. He met with the barons and planned alterations in the law which were put into effect in Ch.1 of the second statute of Westminster 1285. This chapter *(de donis conditionalibus)* recites the grievance and states that such a gift will be treated as an entail (fee taille). In Bracton's words the *modus* of the gift would be respected. There was a good deal of doubt as to the interpretation of this provision, especially as to how long the entail was to hold before it could be barred. Chief Justice Bereford, who had been present in the council when the matter had been discussed, stated that the clause had been carelessly drafted by Chief Justice Hengham and that what he had meant to say was that such gifts should be interpreted as being similar to the maritagium i.e. the entail would be protected for four generations. Before the statute there was a writ of *formedon* (from forma doni, the form of the gift) which could be brought by the original grantor when the estate granted had for some reason failed. This was called *formedon in the ascender*. After the statute a writ of *formedon in the descender* became available. This could be used by the heir in tail to prevent the tenant for life from conveying away the fee simple or enable the remainderman to recover the land if it had been sold. This protection of the entail for four generations was never tested as law; since long before the four generations of the maritagium had passed away a variety of ways of breaking the entail had been devised.

The right of the donor, should the issue fail, is properly called a *reversion* while the right of the person who will take after the preceding life estate or whatever, is called a *remainder*. However, these terms are sometimes confused, and the right of the grantor may be termed a remainder in legal documents and even in text-books. When a clause is inserted to the effect that if the issue of the original grantees failed, some other person or his heirs could become the grantees, this residual estate is called a *conditional remainder* (conditional on the death of someone without heirs). Conditional remainders of one sort or another provided many problems for lawyers. One of the first questions that arose following "de donis" was whether such remaindermen should have the writ of formedon in the remainder to protect their interest in the estate. Ultimately it became the predominant view that they should and so the *fee tail* was established. This battle having been won, the efforts of the legal profession tended to be directed rather toward finding ways to break or bar an entail. (vide infra)

Medieval lawyers also felt obliged to ask where the fee was or (same thing) who would pay homage? At bottom these were questions about who should perform the services and (even more important) how would the incidents apply? The first solution was to say that the fee is in the grantor until the child is born and then it is in the grantees for life. This is the simplest answer from the feudal point of view. Later it was held that the fee is distributed among the heirs, an answer which makes the apportionment of feudal services and incidents almost impossible; but by the time this had happened (in the time of Coke) feudalism and true feudal estates were for the most part .a thing of the past. However, some of the doctrines developed during this emergence from feudal theory, persisted into modern times (like the rule in Shelley's case). The next great set of questions which emerged, focus on conditional grants and how the rights of grantors could be reconciled with those of their family, with established public policies relating to holdings in land and in wealth generally.

§11 *Legal conditional remainders*

In the thirteenth and fourteenth centuries there was a good deal of discussion as to the validity of remainders intended to take effect on future conditions. At first the only such contingency which was acceptable was the death of a person then living (at the time of the grant). So the earliest attempts to go beyond this were grants drawn up specifically to prevent the tenant in tail from conveying the property to a third party. In such grants immediate forfeiture of the land to someone else was to follow any attempt on the part of the life to sell the land or otherwise break the entail. This would have meant that a bona fide purchaser for value would have no title and no right against the heirs even after the purchase was completed. The first case where such a grant was discussed was the case of *Judge Rickhill's settlement* noted by Bracton. It was then considered invalid but in the middle of the fourteenth century came to be regarded as valid. By then entails could be broken in other ways.

A major difficulty (already noted) concerning legal contingent remainders, was that since from the point of view of the medieval legal mind, that it was difficult to see where the fee lay. A future condition then raised the possibility that the previous estate upon which it depended e.g. a life estate, might have disappeared before the contingency actualized (fell in). In such circumstances the fee would, as it was then put, "disappear into the clouds". Various technical devices were permitted to meet this difficulty and allow contingent remainders to stand. Thus eventually it was allowed that if the contingency should *vest* at any time before the precedent estate ended, then the remainder was valid. Thus a grant to A for life and to the first-born son of B, the grant would stand provided B had a son before A died. At the present time, since there is no real concern about the whereabouts of the fee, it is generally held that there can be an interval in time between the end of the previous estate and the vesting of the contingency provided that the gap is not too long. Contingency clauses have also been required (since the case of *Colthurst v. Bejushin* in 1550) that they be not *unreasonable* or *morally repugnant.*

§12 *The rule against perpetuities*

One reason for placing limitations on contingent remainders, besides fears about feudal services and incidents, was that they seemed to be likely to tie up land for an over long period to the detriment of the family and *perhaps* of society as well. Grants of this nature were rendered void in law by the development of the *rule against perpetuities,* first suggested in the *Duke of Norfolk's case* in 1681. Later case law further defined the rule as allowing property to be tied up only for the duration of a life or lives in being and 21 years. This formula itself required a good deal of litigation to define it more precisely, for some people even attempted to make the estate contingent on the lives of a family of turtles which could live in a zoo for several hundred years. The classical rule has therefore been replaced in a significant minority of jurisdictions by other formulae. Some of these are rather general, such as the "wait and see rule" where the contingency will not be declared valid or invalid in advance but considered later at the time of litigation. This does not appear to give much guidance in advance but something like the equitable *cy pres* doctrine (next best thing) used in charitable trusts can be applied. According to this rule trustees charged with trusts which can no longer be carried out (e.g. because the college or church is no more) can apply to the court and have the trust funds reapplied to something as near to (cy pres) the original trust as possible. Similarly the court can see what can be done with a repugnant contingent remainder in order to carry out the wishes of the grantor without interfering with public policies. Another common alternative rule is to allow estates to be tied up for a fixed maximum period of years, e.g.,ninety years.

§13 *Barring the fee tail*

A fee tail was described by Coke as an estate where the fee simple is cut up (taille) between a number of parties, with a life estate to the tenant in tail and remainder to other person or persons e.g. his eldest son. The motive was to keep the family estate intact. The effect of the fee tail was not necessarily to neglect younger sons or daughters. They might be provided for by a charge on the estate, by *inter vivos* gifts to them or in some other way.

The history of the fee tail is a story of the clash between competing interests, those of the grantor in controlling the descent of an estate and the desire of the tenant for life to enlarge his estate and realize money from it by sale or otherwise. Like the eternal struggle between tax collectors and tax evaders, the battle went first one way and then the other. Life tenants and their lawyers invented ingenious ways to bar the entail. A *fine* (a settlement entered on the court rolls) could be used to convey a fee simple free of the limiting conditions; but various measures were soon devised by grantors to counter this e.g. allowing the remainderman to intervene or requiring him to be present *(received)* in court when the settlement was made. A collusive lawsuit could also be employed to effect the same result but again protective devices were provided for the remainderman which made this difficult. The legal warfare dragged on in this manner but the matter was eventually rendered moot by the development of a simple type of family arrangement, called *settlement and resettlement.* In each generation the life tenant in tail persuaded the remainderman, his son now approaching manhood, to agree to a new entailment of the estate whereby the son accepted a future life estate only with the remainder to his son. The motive for accepting this deal was that the new tenant in tail, normally a youth, was promised a substantial allowance in exchange for future hopes of inheriting a fee simple. This would be a very attractive proposition to a young man whose parent, still hale and hearty, might survive for many years and perhaps even out-live him. So effective was this device indeed that many great estates survived intact into the present century only to encounter a more formidable enemy - death duties.

§14 *Uses - the nature of a use*

Attempts have been made to derive the great English institution of the trust from Roman law. It has been seen as a development of the *fidei commission* or the *usufruct* or the idea of *surety* but it is probable that it is not directly related to any of these notions. Nevertheless it did not arise in England *de novo*. A similar institution can be found in the ancient Salic law of the Frankish kingdoms where the *salmon* was virtually a trustee. Something very like a trust is also a common feature of Anglo-Saxon *bocland* (bookland) used for ecclesiastical property.

The origin of the term is the Latin *opus* (work) and it was used in a grant of property to one person to be applied to the affairs *(ad opus)* of some other person or for some purpose (e.g. to build a church or school). In common law, uses were employed for many purposes.

(i) Someone going to the crusades might convey their property to a friend to the use of his wife and family making provision perhaps, in the event of the grantor's death, to have the estate conveyed to the eldest son on his attaining majority etc. or to reconvey it to the grantor should he survive and return.

(ii) An implied *use* was deemed to arise during a sale where the price was paid prior to conveyance of the land to the purchaser. The seller was then considered to hold the property for the use of the buyer i.e. with the duty to convey it to him at the proper time.

(iii) A use was sometimes needed to set up estates other than a fee simple. It was not considered possible for a tenant to change his estate so that the fee simple might have to be conveyed by A to B who was then to reconvey it as directed by the grantor e.g. to A for life and then to the heirs of C.

(iv) Uses were needed by the religious houses of the Franciscans who were not permitted to hold property so that the estate had to reside in a lay person who held them to the use of the order.

§15 The enforcing of uses by chancery

The person who held to the use of another was called the *feofee to use,* since the fee resided with them. The beneficiary on the other hand was called the *cestui que use* (the one who actually gets the benefit). The common law courts would not at first enforce *uses,* for title had passed and recognizing an estate in the foefee to use created problems in feudal theory, just as contingent remainders had done, for it was sometimes difficult to see where the fee was and lords could easily be deprived of services and incidents. The office of the chancellor, however, did enforce them and some rules evolved in the process. The uses had to be clear and certain and the estate on which they rested had likewise to be certain and sure. This meant that there could only be a use on a fee simple. A fee tail was already a sort of trust and a device called a "use upon a use" was considered too problematical and so would not be enforced. Some equitable doctrines were also used in enforcing uses. The *bona fide purchaser for value* was also protected and the uses might not be enforced against them, but the heirs of the feofee to use were strictly bound by the uses. In the Earl of Northumberland's case (1404) the earl had taken part in a rebellion and his lands were liable to forfeiture for treason. The question arose and was debated in parliament as to whether lands which he held to the use of others should also be forfeited. After much debate it was held that they should not.

§16 The Statute of Uses

The problem about feudal dues came to a head in the time of Henry VIII who wanted the incidents of all feudal lands that he could get his hands on since he could not politically afford to raise money by further taxation. The Statute of Uses *executed* the uses i.e. it passed the legal title from the *foefee to use* to the *cestui que use* who was thereupon liable for the feudal services. The feudal incidents (wardship etc.) would also be predicated on the life of the cestui que use as the legal owner. The Statute accomplished much of what the king required for he had to set up a special court (the Court of Wards) to administer the wardships that fell into his hands. It did not however abolish uses altogether for the statute was held not to apply in a number of cases e.g. were there were real trusts to be carried out as opposed to simply holding the title away from the real owner. Likewise it did not apply to estates other than the fee simple and such devices as a *use upon a use* (which had always been held to be no true use) were employed to get around the statute. In fact a whole new body of law arose where fiduciary duties were enforced on legal owners but these were no longer called uses. That term was reserved for those relationships and duties covered by the statute. These were equitable matters and called *trusts*.

ILLUSTRATIVE DOCUMENTS

THE STATUTE OF USES (1536)
27 Hen. VIII, c. 10;

Statutes of the Realm, vol. 111, p. 539 (untr.).

Where by the common laws of this realm, lands, tenements

and hereditaments be not devisable by testament, nor ought to be transferred from one to another but by solemn livery and seisin, matter of record [or] writing sufficient, made bona fide without covin or fraud: yet nevertheless divers and sundry imaginations, subtle inventions and practices have been used whereby the hereditaments of this realm have been conveyed from one to another by fraudulent feoffments, fines, recoveries and other assurances craftily made to secret uses, intents and trusts, and also by wills and testaments sometimes made by nude parols and words, sometimes by signs and tokens, and sometimes by writing, and for the most part made by such persons as be visited with sickness in their extreme agonies and pains, or at such time as they have scantly had any good memory or remembrance, at which times they being provoked by greedy and covetous persons lying in wait about them do many times dispose indiscreetly and unadvisedly their lands and inheritances: by reason whereof, and by occasion of which fraudulent feoffments, fines, recoveries and other like assurances to uses, confidences and trusts, divers and many heirs have been unjustly at sundry times disinherited, the lords have lost their wards, marriages, reliefs, heriots, escheats, aids *pur faire fitz chivaler et pur file marier,* and scantly any person can be certainly assured of any lands by them purchased nor know surely against whom they shall use their actions or executions for their rights, titles and duties; and also men married have lost their tenancies by the curtesy, women their dowers, manifest perjuries by trial of such secret wills and uses have been committed; the king's highness hath lost the profits and advantages of the lands of persons attainted, and of the lands craftily put in feoffments to the uses of aliens born, and also the profits of waste for a year and a day of lands of felons attainted, and the lords their escheats thereof, and many other inconveniences have happened and daily do increase among the king's subjects, to their great trouble and inquietness, and to the utter subversion of the ancient common laws of this realm; and for the extirping and extinguishment of all such subtle practiced feoffments, fines, recoveries, abuses and errors heretofore used and accustomed in this realm, to the subversion of the good and ancient laws of the same, and to the intent that the king's highness or any other his subjects of this realm shall not in any wise hereafter by any means or inventions be deceived, damaged or hurt by reason of such trusts, uses or confidences: it may please the king's royal majesty that it may be enacted by his highness, by the assent of the lords spiritual and temporal and the commons in this present parliament assembled, and by the authority of the same, in manner and form following, that is to say:

That where any person or persons stand or be seised, or at any time hereafter shall happen to be seised, of and in any honours, castles, manors, lands, tenements, rents, services, reversions, remainders or other hereditaments, to the use, confidence or trust of any other person or persons, or of any body politic. by reason of any bargain, sale, feoffment, fine, recovery, covenant, contract, agreement, will, or otherwise, by any manner means whatsoever it be; that in every such case, all and every such person and persons and bodies politic that have or hereafter shall have any such use, confidence or trust in fee simple, fee tail, for term of life or for years, or otherwise, or any use, confidence or trust in remainder or reverter, shall from henceforth stand and be seised. deemed and adjudged in lawful seisin, estate and possession of and in the same honours, castles, manors, lands, tenements, rents, services, reversions, remainders and hereditaments, with their appurtenances, to all intents, constructions, and purposes in the law, of and in such like estates as they had or shall have in use, trust or confidence of or in the same; and that the estate, title, right and possession that was in such person or persons that were, or hereafter shall be, seised of any lands, tenements or hereditaments to the use, confidence or trust of any such person or persons or of any body politic be from henceforth clearly deemed and adjudged to be in him or them that have, or hereafter shall have, such use, confidence or trust, after such quality, manner, form and condition as they had before, in or to the use, confidence or trust that was in them —.

[Concerning jointures:]

And be it further enacted by the authority aforesaid, that whereas divers persons have purchased, or have estate made and conveyed of and in divers lands, tenements and hereditaments unto them and to their wives, and to the heirs of the husband, or to the husband and to the wife and to the heirs of their two bodies begotten, or to the heirs of one of their bodies begotten, or to the husband and to the wife for term of their lives or for term of life of the said wife. or where any such estate or purchase of any lands, tenements or hereditaments hath been or hereafter shall be made to any husband and to his wife in manner and form expressed, or to any other person or persons and to their heirs and assigns to the use and behoof of the said husband and wife or to the use of the wife as is before rehearsed, for the jointure of the wife: that then in every such case, every woman married having such jointure made or hereafter to be made shall not claim nor have title to have any dower of the residue of the lands, tenements or hereditaments that at any time were her said husband's, by whom she hath any such jointure, nor shall demand nor claim her dower of and against them that have the lands and inheritances of her said husband; but if she have no such jointure, then she shall be admitted and enabled to pursue, ha%-e and demand her dower by writ of dower after the due course and order of the common laws of this realm, this act or any law or provision made to the contrary thereof notwithstanding.-- [Preservation of status quo:]

And forasmuch as great ambiguities and doubts may arise of the validity and invalidity of wills heretofore made of any lands, tenements and hereditaments, to the great trouble of the king's subjects, the king's most royal majesty (minding the tranquility and rest of his loving subjects) of his most excellent and accustomed goodness is pleased and contented that it be enacted by the authority of this pre parliament that all manner true and just wills and testaments heretofore made by person or persons deceased, or that shall decease before the first day of May that shall be in the year of our Lord God 1536, of any lands, tenements or other hereditaments, shall be taken and accepted good and effectual in the law. after fashion, manner and form as they were commonly taken and used at any time w 40 years next afore the making of this act; anything contained in this act or in the preamble thereof, or any opinion of the common law to the contrary thereof,' notwithstanding

.

THE STATUTE OF ENROLMENTS (1536)
27 Hen. VIII, c. 16;
Statutes of the Realm, vol. 111, p. 549.

Be it enacted by the authority of this present parliament that from the last of July which shall be in the year of our Lord God 1536 no manors, lands, tenem or other hereditaments shall pass, alter or change from one to another whereby any estate of inheritance or freehold shall be made or take effect in any person or persons, or any use thereof to be made by reason only of any bargain and sale thereof, except the same bargain and sale be made by writing indented, sealed, enrolled in one of the king's courts of record at Westminster; or else within the s county or counties where the same manors, lands or tenements so bargained and sold lie or be, before the *custos rotulorum* and the justices of the peace and the of the peace of the same county or counties, or two of them at the least, whereof clerk of the peace to be one, and the same enrotment to be had and made within months next after the date of the same writings indented ... Provided always that [neither] this act, nor anything therein contained. extend to any manner lands, tenements or hereditaments lying or being within any city, borough or town corpor within this realm. wherein the mayors, recorders, chamberlains, bailiffs or other o or officers have authority or have lawfully used to enrol any evidences, deeds or writings within their precinct or limits. anything in this act contained to the contrary notwithstanding.

CHAPTER SEVEN
INHERITANCE

§1. The effects of the Norman conquest on inheritance

William the conqueror in the charter which he issued at the beginning of his reign as King of England announced " I will that every child shall be his father's heir". This may have been intended to reassure his new subjects that their property would be secured to their descendants but there were a number of loopholes in the promise.

(i) Many of his new subjects would forfeit their lands and goods for opposing the King.

(ii) Since land holdings were to be reorganized upon feudal lines the fee would be held of a Norman lord who might gain the land through escheat or some other incident and regrant it to someone else.

(iii) Finally, during the 12th century, the Norman rule determining descent of land by primogeniture would largely replace older systems where it was shared among all the sons or distributed on some other customary principle. The only exception to this would be property in the larger towns (boroughs) which, as commercial centers, were able to maintain their own courts and their own customs.

§2 The rules of descent

The Anglo-Saxon rules of inheritance only required one thing, identifying the group among whom the inheritance should be divided (more or less in equal parts). The continental system had two stages. First the group of possible heirs, the *parentela,* was outlined and then the heir was selected from within it. The identification of the appropriate parentela followed rules which apply clearly and simply in most cases.

(i) The first principle is that descendants are preferred to ascendants. Thus the children, grandchildren etc. of the deceased are considered first.

(ii) If there are no direct descendants the second parentela is identified by considering the descendants of the father of the deceased i.e. brothers, sisters, nieces and nephews.

(iii) If there are no descendants of the father of the deceased then the senior parentela is consulted, i.e. the descendants of the grandfather of the deceased. This would comprise uncles, aunts, cousins, etc.

(iv) If all of the above parentelic groups fail to produce a potential heir, the deceased would be deemed to be without heirs and the land would revert to the grantor.

Determining who, among all the members of the appropriate parentela, should be the heir could be a more difficult matter and the rules varied somewhat in different countries.

(i)   Males would normally take before females. descendants from the male at the head of each parentela were also preferred to those claiming collateral descent through the female

(ii)   There was some difference as to whether ascendants, the father or grandfather of the deceased, could inherit. In Normandy inheritance could pass to the head of a parentela in the absence of descendants but in Italy and in England this was not so. The reason offered by historians for this denial was that one could not be both lord and heir. Parents, working with primogeniture, granted land to younger sons etc. thus becoming their feudal lord. It was not thought proper on the death of such children that the land should revert to the grantor but to follow the rules of descent for the grantee i.e. go to the next parentela.

(iii)   Another disputed question was whether a descendant who had predeceased the holder of the land in question could be *represented* by his son. The general view was, or came to be, that the deceased son could be represented by the grandson. This was often ensured by the tenant persuading his immediate lord to take homage from the tenant's eldest son which made the grandson the heir should the son predecease the father. The settling of the representation question in favor of the grandson was long delayed by the *casus regis* i.e. the case of Prince John who succeeded his brother King Richard I by seizing the throne though children of his older brother Geoffrey were still alive. Eleanor, daughter of Geoffrey was indeed held captive until her death without issue to ensure the succession. It was difficult in these circumstances, which lasted well into the reign of John's son Henry III, for judges to prefer a nephew to his uncle in a dispute ever title to land. Eventually the theory of representation triumphed but since land had by then become freely alienable and could be disposed of by will the question was largely moot. Generally however for most purposes children will inherit their dead parents share.

(iv) The question of the half blood was also troublesome. The difficulty in admitting the half blood as heirs may have stemmed from the admitted impropriety of giving property derived from the family of the first wife to children by a second wife. In one early case the children of the half blood were excluded because the property in question did not derive from the common parent. In most cases however the children of the half blood were excluded regardless of which parent had owned the land. The reasons for this are obscure and seem to have derived from the doctrine of primogeniture, for in

Germanic tribes where the children shared in the land the half-blood were treated equally with the others. In the one case where this equal sharing or *parcenage* survived (i.e. daughters inheriting from their mother) the females inherited equally even though the land did not derive from a common parent. Also if one died intestate the other took all, not by heritance but because *co-parceners* were considered as a single heir.

§3   *Troublesome technicalities affecting inheritance of land*

There were a number of other knotty problems connected with inheritance of land. The heir, for instance, did not take automatically but had to enter on the land and one who entered before the heir was committing no disseisin. This requirement was gradually eroded however and by the fifteenth century (when Littleton wrote his treatise on Tenures) the heir was deemed to have a freehold. on the death of the testator even though he had not entered. Thus a widow could claim dower even if her husband had died before he could enter on the inherited land.

The responsibility of the heir for the debts of the deceased was another troublesome matter and the medieval rule was that, absent special debts, there was no liability. On the other hand all sorts of other onerous duties of a feudal nature did devolve on the heir so that conveyancers used their ingenuity to disguise the heir as a purchaser or *cestui que use* or anything other than the heir. These problems were largely moot by the 16th century since land became freely devisable in 1540. They were finally settled in England by legislative reforms in the 19th century. The Inheritance Act of 1833 abolished *seisina facit stipitem* (it is being seized that makes the heir) and also allowed inheritance in the ascendant and by the half blood. By the Land Transfer Act of 1887 real and personal property were made to descend by the same rules and the personal representative took all properties and held them on trust for the heir or heirs subject to the liabilities of the deceased to his creditors.

§4   *Descent of personal property and intestacy*

Personal property was treated quite differently from land so far as inheritance was concerned. This has sometimes been ascribed to the fact that the King's courts controlled the descent of land while inheritance of personal property was handled by the Church. However, the difference between the two far antedates this divided jurisdiction and seems to depend on some real perceived difference between the two, such as that the land belonged to the family while personalty was ones own.

In Anglo-Saxon times a man's goods were distributed in accordance with a customary scheme where the wife (provided she had borne her husband a child) was entitled to half of his goods and the rest was divided among the children. However, wills were common and indeed it was considered negligence to die intestate. If someone died without disposing of his goods the estate was administered by his lord who distributed them according to the customary mode and took the best beast as a *heriot* for his trouble. The Conqueror did not at first disturb this arrangement but by the time of Glanville intestacy had become a grave ecclesiastical offense disapproved also by the Crown and was punishable in some instances by forfeiture of goods. The reason for the Church's attitude was that it was considered essential that some charitable bequest should be made by someone about to meet their maker. Approximately one third of ones personal goods were considered to be the soul's share (the dead man's share) which would be given to the poor or to a school or to the church or used for some other charitable purpose. This duty was normally fulfilled by making a *nuncupative will,* spoken to the priest in the presence of lay witnesses. In short it was an essential part of preparation for dying. Failure to carry out this duty suggested that the departed had *died desperate,* without, and perhaps refusing, the last rites of the Church (*desperant* in Norman French meant without hope).

§5 *Ecclesiastical jurisdiction over descent of persona goods*

In the rural setting the estate would in most cases be land and so the heir would naturally recover. In the towns wealth would normally be mainly in goods and it was here that the crown began to assert a right to forfeiture on intestacy. Such claims by the crown were unpopular and were gradually abandoned. Magna Carta, e.g., insisted that intestacy ought not to prejudice the family of the deceased. From this point on the Church in the person of the bishop of the diocese becomes the administrator and the term "ordinary' refers to an ordained clergyman. The usual practice however was that the ordinary appoint a deputy as administrator to pay debts and distribute the goods of the deceased in a suitable manner, usually one third to the widow, one third to the children and the remaining third being disposed as the dead man's or soul's share. The statute of Westminster II (1285) allowed the ordinary to be sued by creditors and a later statute dealt with a serious problem of that time by allowing the ordinary to sue as the representative of the deceased's estate. This system operated satisfactorily so long as the ecclesiastical courts were allowed to function; but from the late fifteenth century on there was increasing interference with these by the common law courts and in the sixteenth century they were reduced to complete impotence by the issuance of the writ of prohibition from King's Bench. The administrator in these circumstances could not be compelled to distribute the property of the estate. A particularly notorious case in 1666 brought matters to a head and after a great deal of discussion the *Statute of Distributions* was passed in 1670. This act allowed the ordinary to compel administrators to distribute but the common law courts were still able to obstruct the process so that gradually jurisdiction in these matters passed into the hands of Chancery. The importance of this statute is that it established a number of schemes and systems of distribution. The dead man's part disappeared, one third went to the widow and two thirds to the children. A deceased child could be represented by the grandchildren, and in the absence of children, the widow took half and the rest went to the next of kin.

If there was not e widow the next of kin took all. The medieval custom of the borough of London, known the *hotch-pot,* was introduced by this statute to ensure equal distribution among the family of the deceased. Later, further amendments were made by case law and statute to allow the half blood and ascendants to share with the brothers and sisters as next of kin.

§6 *Wills*

The earliest written wills from Anglo-Saxon times are in the vernacular not Latin. Anglo-Saxon charters and landbook deeds were in polished Latin (diplomatic Latin) but ordinary wills were much cruder and seem indeed to be the minutes of an oral transaction where the testator in the presence of witnesses said his say (quaeth his quide), which was the original for our term to *bequeath.* There was a good deal of flexibility as to how a will should operate. In some cases it was a solemn promise, in others it was more like a gift conditional upon a future event (the death of the testator). In some cases it was treated like a gift *inter vivos* with the testator reserving the use of the gift for the remainder of his life. All of these unlike the modern will, were deemed irrevocable since, even if it was only a promise, it clearly ought to be honored.

Making other people honor the testator's wishes was a different and often a more difficult matter. It was common to invoke hearty curses on anyone who obstructed the execution of the will, but the help of a powerful or influential patron or *mund* (protector) was sometimes sought to ensure that the wishes of the testator were put into effect.

The Anglo-Saxon will was closely associated with the Church in all its workings. The tripartite division of goods was widely used in Germanic society where the soul's part was burned or buried with the deceased, presumably for their use in the other world. With the christianization of the Germanic invaders of Britain, it was thought that the soul's part could be put to better uses. Its disposition became closely associated, as was mentioned earlier, with preparation for departure from this life and so the clergy would naturally be consulted and might well make suggestions as to how this good work should be carried out.

After the conquest the Anglo-Saxon will seems to have declined in importance. In strict feudal theory land could not be devised or bequeathed. Even as feudalism and feudal practice declined, land was not at first willed but rather transferred during the lifetime of the tenant by means of such devices as a gift *inter vivos* with a use to the grantor for life. However, towns which had borough charters operated according to different rules. Here land was freely devisable (it was not usually held in military tenure but in what was called "borough English"). Also wealth in forms other than land (goods and money) would be more likely to exist. As mercantile centers, the towns were exposed to continental practices based on Civil and Canon law. The Roman testament and the institution of the executor thus naturally came into the borough courts and of course into the ecclesiastical courts as the Church took jurisdiction over the inheritance of chattels. The executor was necessary to ensure that the charitable bequests of the "soul's part " were carried out for it was hardly in the interest of the heirs to do this. The old protector or mund who carried out these duties became invested with the character of the executor in Roman law and during the thirteenth century it was also recognized (by importation of Roman Law doctrines) that the testament was neither a contract nor a gift but was revokable at any time. Written wills became much more common during this period although the old *novissima verba* (famous last words) spoken in the presence of a priest would give rise to a valid set of bequests. However, the influence of the church at the time of death was widely distrusted and the priest was expected to be accompanied by two or more lay persons. Seals were used rather than signatures.

§7   *The Statute of Wills*

The Statute of Wills (1540) required that a devise of land should be written, signed and witnessed by three or four credible witnesses. This was not extended to wills generally until 1837. The term credible gave rise to problems. One who was a legatee was an interested party and so held not to be credible. At first this was likely to make the entire will void for lack of enough witnesses and an act of 1752 was required to make the bequest void but the will valid. What the witnesses were attesting was also a matter that needed a good deal of amplification by the courts. They were eventually held to be certifying that it was indeed the testator who signed the will and that nothing grossly improper was going on.

§8 *Jurisdictional conflicts and their effect on probate*

The local bishop at first merely acted to appoint the executor and only became actively involved if there was some dispute. The requirement that all wills be probated in the ecclesiastical courts, whether disputed or not, followed from this and the See of Canterbury acquired jurisdiction when there was considerable property in more than one diocese. This right to probate wills remained in the ecclesiastical courts until the new Court of Probate was established in 1857. However, many matters, required the assistance of the common law courts. Debts might need to be collected by the executor or the executors might need to be sued in debt. If there were several executors they could take advantage of the essoins (excuses) of common law and take sick in turn (fourcher) to delay collection in the common law courts. The common law courts, as was mentioned earlier, could and did obstruct the ecclesiastical courts all through the middle ages and by the reign of Queen Elizabeth had reduced them to impotence, although they continued to function in some matters right into the nineteenth century. Since the common law courts could e.g. prevent the ecclesiastical courts from acting on a bond (typically entered into by an executor to pay debts or discharge trusts) an unconscionable executor might simply keep the inheritance. Such cases naturally gravitated into the court of Chancery. In developing jurisdiction over wills the chancery, like the church courts before it, used the Roman law of the *testamentum*.

§9   *Balancing the rights of testator and family*

Before the Norman conquest and until the royal courts began to change the law of the land, customary schemes of distribution both of land and chattels looked after the interests of the family. The widow had her share, the sons divided the land, chattels were divided equally and the maritagium was a gift given as dowry to a daughter on marriage. An attempt by an individual to interfere with this arrangement by gift or bequest was at first illegal and indeed the appropriate shares of the family were termed the *legitim* i.e. what was rightfully theirs and could not be taken from them by the testator. The royal courts did not however recognize this principle and as the ecclesiastical courts were progressively stripped of their effectiveness by King's Bench during the middle ages, the action *de rationabili parte* (reasonable partition) which had formerly been available against heirs or executors who ignored legitim, fell into disuse and indeed was not allowed in the common law courts. Even in the boroughs where older customs tended to survive, legitim was replaced by more or less complete freedom of the testator to do what he wished with his own property. This change in the boroughs was motivated apparently by the reluctance of wealthy persons to become freedmen of those boroughs if they were denied freedom of testation. Some respect for the old system however lingered and some doubts about complete freedom of testation persisted. Thus lawyers, drafting wills for persons who wished to disinherit their family, frequently "cut them off with a shilling" apparently under the notion that otherwise the will might be upset as a *testamentum inofficiosum* (invalid will). This was indeed *true* in Europe where some provision for the family was an essential part of a valid will. Eventually the legislature had to intervene and at least maintenance grants were required. This was far short of the principle of legitim and the grants did not need to be made in all cases, but it was a start and later acts, both in England and America, have turned the clock back more or less to the ancient system except that the dead man's part has been removed.

CHAPTER EIGHT
TORTS

§1 Development of the Law of Torts

Actions for civil wrongs of various *kinds* (complaints) were addressed in county and local courts before the Norman conquest and continued to be heard there for centuries. They were called trespasses (*transgressiones* in Latin) and some of the larger baronial courts even had a writ of trespass.

Civil complaints (as opposed to demands) can be roughly divided into three groups; *intentional torts* brought under a writ of trespass, *negligence actions* brought under the action in the case and some *special actions* such as deceit, defamation, nuisance and so on. Both intentional and negligent torts have been impliedly considered earlier in Ch.2, dealing with the forms of action at common law and especially with the actions of trespass and trespass on the case. Trespass and case were used interchangeably throughout the later middle ages and only came to be considered distinct from one another in the nineteenth century. There had always been a tendency in the common law to feel that each wrong had its proper writ and vice versa, i.e. that the writs should not overlap in their operation. In the early nineteenth century trespass was first held to lie properly for direct injuries, as when I strike someone with my fist or a weapon, whereas case lay for indirect injuries as when I carelessly leave a log lying on a road and someone falls over it at night. After 1825 it began to be said that the difference lay in the motive for the wrong, intentional acts or reckless conduct (which was held to amount to the same thing) should be brought under trespass while merely negligent harms would come under trespass on the case. Something more will be said about the action for negligence in §6 infra and it will also be noted how the procedural advantages of the trespass action made it the preferred way of dealing with all sorts of problems including disputes about contracts or title to land. The same procedural advantages encouraged adaptation and the development of torts actions in a number of situations such as fraud and defamation where there was no personal injury or property damage. The growth of the law of torts has been, like many other remedies a tortuous and complicated development.

§2 The action of deceit

The action of deceit has a long history (it will be mentioned later in relation to contract). It was an old action in communal and borough courts. It was available in a broad variety of cases but most commonly used in relation to sale of goods. In borough courts one who knowingly purveyed bad fish or bad bread could be fined and might also be liable for compensatory damages to the person deceived. When this action came into the Royal courts (after the requirement for a specific injury against the crown was dropped) it was most commonly used in warranty cases. But the false warrantor was no longer fined and the offense aspect faded into the background. As a result fraud and innocent misrepresentation were treated alike; the matter was really one of contract and promisors were not allowed to plead in defense that they acted honestly. True fraud in contracts was remedied in Chancery and also in Star Chamber when that was established by the Tudors. The action on the case for deceit could, however, be used in non-contractual cases in which case fraud might be alleged. It lay for instance for cheating at cards[2] and one who misrepresented himself as a person to whom a sum of money was due could be sued in an action on the case for deceit.[3] The action in deceit was also used to recover on what we would describe as implied warranties. Thus a seller impliedly warranted that he had title and those who sold

---

[2] *Baxter v Woodyard and Orbit* (1605) Moore K.B 776
[3] *Thompson v Gardner* (1597) Moor e K.B., 538

food for immediate consumption warranted it to be fit to eat. Absent an express or implied warranty there was a considerable reluctance on the part of the courts to allow an action for misrepresentation in a contract of sale. In the famous case of *Chandelor v. Lopus*[4] (1603) the defendant, a dealer in precious stones, represented to the plaintiff that a certain stone was a "bezoar", a stone formed in an animal's stomach which was believed to have healing properties. The dealer's untrue statement fell short of a warranty but he was held liable because he had made it knowing (sciens) that it was false. The courts here approached but fell back from the idea that there could be a torts action based on fraud. There are two reports of this case (there may have been two actions) and they do not agree in every particular. Both however note the uneasiness of the bench at this departure from *caveat emptor*. Thereafter *scientia* ceases to be alleged in such cases and absent a warranty there would be no recovery. But in the famous case of *Pasley v. Freeman* in 1789 the tort of deceit for knowingly (or recklessly) false statements, whether associated with contract or not, was finally established. This has been described by many writers as the invention of a tort but it was really the restoration of an old one, one that had been lost as the Royal courts replaced the customary ones. Maitland remarks of such developments that principles eventually avenge themselves.

§3   *The tort of conversion*

The term conversion was used in local courts to describe a bailiff or trustee converting moneys, which they held for another, to their own use. If an executor used the testator's estate for his own purposes he could be sued in the action of account (a *praecipe* similar to *debt/detinue*) and made to repay the moneys misused. He would also as a punishment be made to pay the debts of the estate out of his own money if that should prove necessary. The modern action of *conversion* developed out of *detinue* brought against a bailee. If the bailed property was

---

[4] *Chandelor v Lopus* Cro. Jac.,4

merely damaged the appropriate action would be an action on the case for negligence or perhaps an assumpsit. If however the property was lost or destroyed the proper action was detinue and the burden of proving that the loss was accidental was on defendant (he had to wage his law). In 1472 a plaintiff tried to bring an action on the case against a bailee and probably failed. One year later however in *the carriers case* where the defendant "broke bulk" he was held liable for its full value when it was afterwards destroyed. Later cases were brought against sub-bailees where the action of detinue strictly speaking would not lie. In these cases it was customary to say that they had come to the hand *(devenit ad manus)*[5] of the defendant which was known as the count in *trover.* But it was difficult to bring cases in bailment other than in detinue with wager of law as a defense. If however it could be alleged that the property had been altered then this might be alleged as more than mere damage and indeed could be considered a separate wrong similar to the promise to pay subsequent to a debt. Such pleas were made in the late 15th century where one had broken up silver cups and another had made cloth of gold into a suit. In this last case the Roman Law action of *specificatio* was mentioned which may be the origin of our action on the case for conversion but in neither case was the court able to make up its mind. By the early 1600s however it was said that conversion ended bailment and that the action on the case would lie. From this point on the action of detinue was obsolete unless one wished to use it. Even if there had been a genuine bailment this would not prevent the action on the case for conversion from being brought and a conversion would be inferred if the defendant had either used the property as his own or had so altered it that it could not be returned in its original form (the Roman specificatio). But it took many years and many cases to determine the circumstances in which either of these two types of conversion (use or alteration) could be inferred with any certainty. The problem also remained as to whether the owner could follow the property into the hands of third parties *(mobilia non habent sequelam).* Eventually it was decided to use

---

[2] *Thompson v. Gardner* (1597), Moore K.B. 538

another maxim *(nemo dat qui non habet)* so that title did not pass and converted property could be followed provided it had not been purchased in market overt. Liability in conversion could also be applied to all intermediate persons who had sold or otherwise disposed of the property even though they did so innocently.

§4 *Defamation*

Cases of defamation, including slander of goods and title, were quite common in local courts where the defamer was punished and the plaintiff compensated for the wrong. But in the Royal courts cases alleging defamation were uncommon before 1500. Until this time the Royal judges considered defamation to be largely a matter for the ecclesiastical authorities and it has been remarked that when they began to hear select cases of defamation they took over the vocabulary and concepts of the Church courts. In the Church courts excommunication was pronounced against those who maliciously (malitia = bad motive) imputed crimes to persons of good reputation so that they had to clear themselves by compurgation or were punished in some other way. The temporal authorities were concerned that this might be used against indictors and a Statute of 1327 expressly forbade the haling of indictors before Church courts on charges of defamation. Otherwise the common law courts do not seem to have minded even when the allegations were of temporal crimes and damages were awarded. The Church was only supposed to exact spiritual penalties but in fact the threat of excommunication could be used to persuade the defendant to make restitution or offer compensation, both of which might in a sense be considered to be damages. There were some cases, however, where the ecclesiastical remedies were not available and the Royal courts had to step in. The earliest of these involved allegations that the plaintiff was a villein *(nativus)* i.e. belonged to someone as a serf and so could not trade for his own benefit. It was not a crime in any sense to be a villein so this was not defamation as defined by Church law. The writ,

126

which could be in trespass, used words taken from the ecclesiastical legal vocabulary. In one case of 1511 it is alleged:

That the plaintiff who was esteemed of good reputation by good and grave men had been injured by the defendant who schemed wrongly (i.e. with malice or *malitia*) to take away the name and estate of the plaintiff by naming him *nativus*. On a certain day and date he pronounced these words in English.

"Thou knave, thou art Sir John Rysley's bondman and somme of these days he will seize thy body and thy goods" whereby the plaintiff is widely harmed in his estate, name and in his lawful business of buying selling and dealing with honourable persons whereof he says that he has suffered damage to the value of £20.

Most of the elements of the modern tort of defamation can be seen in this complaint.

It was also felt that spiritual sanctions were not enough where there was temporal loss, for a hardy defendant might choose to endure spiritual sanctions rather than compensate his victim. So the Royal courts began to hear cases e.g., where a woman was accused of having an illegitimate child and thereby had lost a marriage or where a charge of illegitimacy (or legitimacy in an older brother) might produce *disherison*. In Richard Hunne's case (1513) a merchant was falsely declared to be a heretic and excommunicated by the parish priest. He brought an action in the Royal courts as his business was affected since other merchants feared to deal with an excommunicated person. He also brought an action in *praemunire to* prevent an ecclesiastical appeal to Rome.

From such cases the idea emerged that temporal damage arising from a defamatory statement might be actionable as such in the Royal courts and the common categories, imputation of a serious crime, professional disparagement, communicable disease and sexual misconduct in a woman became standardized as *slander per se*. Otherwise, a man could only recover if he had suffered temporal damage and allegations of incompetence were not considered to compromise professional reputation, moral unfitness must be averred. An attorney for instance recovered for the statement "he is the falsest knave in England and would cut thy throat".

It would seem that earlier fears that there would be a flood of such cases were justified and the Royal courts in the seventeenth century began to back off defamation, making it harder to recover. One way in which this was done was by the *mitior sensus* (the better interpretation) rule. This was that if a statement could be interpreted in a non-defamatory sense it would be. Thus the statement "thou hast stolen by the road side" could mean that you had come on someone unawares and so would not be actionable. And "he has as much law as my horse" said of a lawyer was actionable since the horse is an irrational being but to say "he knows no more law than X", would not be deemed defamatory unless it was shown how much law X in fact knew. These roundabout ways of discouraging over-ready recourse to litigation as a method of avenging insults thus produced a number of detailed rules most which have been overturned.

§5 *Libel*

Libel takes its origin in the interest of the State in defamation. Fifteenth century statutes forbade the publication of discreditable charges against important people (magnates) and a few civil cases were brought on these statutes. Criminal action for defamation however began with the establishment of Star Chamber at the end of the fifteenth century. The business of this court was public order and since printed defamation in those times frequently led to a violent response, those convicted would be punished and redress might be ordered for the victim. Libel included not only printed pamphlets but the use of signs and symbols, e.g. chalking a gallows on the victim's door or reading a pamphlet out loud in public. Repeating the libelous words of another person also constituted libel. Truth was at first no defense since "the more truth the greater the libel" i.e. more public unrest.

Star chamber is no more, but many of its rules entered into the law of defamation both in England and in the United States. So both malice and damage were presumed in libel and did not have to be proved. However, the truth of the allegations could later be pleaded as a defense. The case which firmly established libel as an action in common law was *Thorley v. Lord Kerry* where an action for libel was allowed for abuse such as would bring someone into *hatred contempt and ridicule.* The court remarked that since public order was no longer an issue in such cases, there *ought* to be no difference between libel and slander and malice and damage should be proved in either action if the case did not fall into the *per se* categories of slander. Nevertheless it was felt that the distinction between libel and slander had become settled law and should not be changed. The matter has rested thus in England till this day. In the US following a series of constitutional cases e.g. *Gerz v. Welch* the distinction between libel and slander seemed abolished [6].

§6 Negligence

The action in *negligence is* in a sense very modem. In England it may only really have come into existence in the snail in the bottle case (*Donaghue v. Stevenson*) in 1959. In another sense it is very old having been present in essence since the development of the action on the case with its requirement that the plaintiff show fault in the defendant. But the term negligence was not used as a technical term referring to a cause of action until late in the nineteenth century. Before

---

[6] 414 US 423 (1974). However subsequent cases have differed from the clear reasoning of the court in *Gerz v Welch* and the differences between libel and slander remain.

that time it might be used to indicate the fact that the defendant had *neglected* something as when a law suit was described as an action on the case for negligence (non-feasance) as opposed to misfeasance. It is only in the twentieth century that the tort of negligence, with its own proper elements[7], has been seen as a cause of action.

Actions alleging negligence were complicated by the survival of the old trespass action after 1370 when a breach of the peace no longer needed to be alleged and the actual facts could be pleaded in the "cum" clause. It was felt desirable that each case should be brought under its proper writ. [See §1] This presented plaintiffs' lawyers arguing at Westminster with something of a dilemma, since they might not know the facts until they were determined later at *nisi prius* by the jury. Suppose that the case concerns a boat ramming into a dock and damaging it and that the plaintiff finds that the owner was at the tiller steering it. Trespass would then seem appropriate since the injury was direct. But when the only answer to trespass is the general denial, special facts will not be pleaded till nisi prius when it is too late to change the plea. In one case the plaintiff later found out that a sudden gust of wind had driven the boat into the dock and, since the injury was then indirect, case was the proper writ and trespass was the wrong one.

After 1833 either writ was allowable (they were considered interchangeable) for a while. Finally trespass was deemed the appropriate writ for intentional torts and case for negligently inflicted injuries. Yet even then case was fragmented up into all sorts of particular circumstances each with its own peculiarities such as professional negligence etc. This process has continued right up to the present. Finding and evaluating fault in all these sub-species of negligence is rapidly becoming too difficult for juries and several jurisdictions have replaced some forms of negligence by no-fault systems of

---

[7] I.e. Duty, breach of duty, cusation and damage.

compensation. Whether this trend will continue across the board remains to be seen.

CHAPTER NINE
CONTRACTS

§1 Contract in the Anglo-Saxon period

There were three formal contracts in pre-Norman England, the marriage contract, the contract to pay compensation to the family following a homicide and the contractual arrangements made to ensure that a defendant turned up in court. These and all other transactions of a contractual nature were based on a formal promise *(borh)* and evidenced by a formal act or something given in pledge *(wed)*. A ring was commonly given as pledge in a promise to marry hence the term wedding.

All sorts of things could be treated as a wed. One could give any small item or ones hand (let's shake on it). Bargains for instance could be formalized by a small coin and a drink and this is still the custom in rural fairs and markets in Europe. Under ecclesiastical influence the wed could be ones hope of salvation (regarded as a possession and a thing) and it could even be formally handed over into the possession of the sheriff. The church tried to claim jurisdiction over the entire contract if this was done, but Henry II stoutly resisted this and by the Constitutions of Clarendon (1164 a.d.) it was laid down that the contract was to be enforced by the secular courts although the church could if they so desired punish the offender for the false promise. This allows room for indirect enforcement and Church/State conflict in this matter still remained (Edward I had to deal with it the late 13th century) but generally the law of contracts was a matter for state courts. Third party *sureties* were often included. These held the wed (like stake-holders in a wager) and were also responsible for ensuring that the promisor carried out his obligations. Thus they were like bail bondsmen and that indeed is what they were in a contract to appear in court. The terms "body for body" are indeed still used in releasing someone on bail although it is no longer necessary for the bail bondsman to incur the penalty of the defaulting defendant.

The written contract under seal or obligation (lat. *obligatio*) does not appear till after the conquest and was probably therefore a continental import. The sealed document was probably regarded as the solemn wed handed over to the promisee. The sealed document (deed) remained the most solemn kind of contractual evidence during the middle ages and tended therefore to be used seldom and only in very special circumstances. A major factor in its decline was the circumstance that fewer and fewer people had seals although one could use, with permission, the seal of another person. There was no real action of covenant, as there was an action in trespass or debt. Covenants were enforced as solemn promises or treated as the best possible evidence of a debt or other obligation. Wager of law did not avail against a deed.

§2 *The use of debt/detinue*

Commerce was very limited in the middle ages, the two main business transactions being loans and sales, with bailments making up a distant third. It is now known that the local courts had writs of debt and that much of the procedure of the action of debt in the royal courts was taken over from these. In the royal courts the action of debt was initiated by a writ ordering the local court to see to it that A restored to B the money owed i.e. a *praecipe quod reddat* [See Ch.2 §3]. A *praecipe* was of course used to recover land in which case it was known as the *writ of right.* If it was used to put someone off land that was rightfully yours, it was called a *writ of entry.* When the thing demanded was not money or land but cattle unlawfully distrained or property left on bail or purchased goods which had not been delivered, then the action was known as *detinue* This was not a separate action, it was identical with the action of debt and was frequently called debt, or debt in the detinue. The general issue or general denial would differ on the words. The "non debitur" in debt became "non detinet" in detinue. Special pleas (exceptions) are not found in the rolls for the simple reason that they were not allowed. It was felt that these would be confusing to the juries at *nisi prius* and so only the general issue could be pleaded; any excuses which the defendant chose to make could be taken into the reckoning by the jury. Thus the finding of the jury might be "non detinet" in a case where a horse was indeed bailed but had been washed away and drowned in a flood without fault on the part of the bailee, or if the debtor had worked for the creditor to pay off the debt their finding be "non debitur" i.e. no money owed. The failure of the plea rolls to record special circumstances should not then be taken to mean that they were not heard or considered.

§3 *Problems of proving a debt and choosing a court*

The main problem in actions of debt was proof of the debt. The best evidence of course was the sealed document but absent this, a debt could be proved in other ways. In larger borough courts sticks could be notched, and cross-notched as the debt was paid. If the promise was given in open market this would also be good evidence. If however the matter boiled down to the word of the parties and their suit (people who supported their claim) then the defendant could resort to warranty of oath. This was reasonably effective in the local and borough courts where the parties were known; it might then be very difficult for a rogue to find enough people of good reputation to back up his sworn testimony. In London, however, oath helpers could be hired right outside the Court of Common Pleas. It is therefore easy to understand why most actions of debt were brought in local courts right into the sixteenth century even though a royal remedy had been available since the early 1300s. However if the transaction had been important enough to warrant a deed then the action would most likely be brought in the royal court since the sheriff could be sent to bring in the defendant (or declare him an outlaw if he could not be found) and after judgement had been pronounced the defaulting debtor could be committed to prison until the debt was paid (a very old procedure mentioned in the Bible).

There were occasionally very important promises where failure to perform might result in significant harm, such as failure to build a dam or to build up an embankment beside a river to prevent spring flooding. Such contracts could be protected by a conditional deed where an amount which would cover the damage would be due (without reasons or excuses) unless the work was completed satisfactorily and in time. Later as we shall see recovery could be had under a form of trespass writ without a deed.

In the time of Glanville (late 12th century) a debt could also be made secure by a collusive court proceeding where it became a *debt of record* which functioned in much the same way as a sealed covenant. Debts to Jewish moneylenders were enrolled separately (in the Jewish chest) and enforced in the Royal courts as a debt of record. But the Jews were banished from England by king Edward I towards the end of the thirteenth century.

Payment for goods or services rendered was also considered a debt but required that something should have been done or handed over by the plaintiff; this something was known as the *quid pro quo* (something given in exchange for something). In the Royal courts the QPQ had to be goods or money. A bare promise could be enforced in a suretyship agreement but otherwise not. Sticks and handshakes and formal handing over of ones hope of salvation would not do. Church courts backed up such agreements with ecclesiastical sanctions fitfully, but generally they were not enforceable contracts as we would understand those terms. It should also be mentioned that in certain circumstances Chancery might take a hand in the proceedings. This could only occur of course if legal remedies had failed (equity follows the law) but one could for instance allege that the debtor had fraudulently waged (or was about to wage) his law and the chancery might compel payment.

§4 *The action of account*

The action of account was available in the 12th century and was for the most part used by feudal lords against their stewards. It came also to be used between partners and, as uses became more popular, the *cestui qui use* (beneficiary) could bring this action against the *feoffee to use* (trustee). Generally its development as a contract remedy was limited by the requirement that there be some recognized relationship between the parties such as the above. This action, like debt/detinue, was a *praecipe quod reddat.* Once it was brought, two auditors were proposed by the plaintiff. If these were not agreed to by the defendant the court would appoint them. These had the right (known as an equity) to disallow any item in the accounts and the amount due was reckoned a judgement debt. They could indeed in the thirteenth century hale the accountant (the one responding in the action of account) to prison and have them incarcerated. Later, when sharp traders used their own clerks as pseudo-auditors (the earlier auditors seem to have been substantial persons) it was deemed necessary to follow up the accounting with an action of debt if amounts owing by the accountant were not paid.

It is clear that the royal courts did much less business in these areas than the local courts, and that local justice was deemed satisfactory for most purposes until the sixteenth century. This was especially the case in borough courts and statutory mercantile and staple courts which had effective means of enforcing agreements (usually on showing that earnest money had been paid over). The advantage of the royal court was ease in getting the defendant into court and the use of the machinery of state to collect the debt. The amount owing had to exceed forty shillings but inflation made this less important. The real problem was that wager of law attached to the writ of debt in the local setting. This problem was avoided by developing a contract remedy based on trespass

§5 *The trespass actions as contractual remedies*

There was a trespass action available in local courts and its procedure was used as the basis of the Royal action, which alleged a breach of the King's peace. The King's peace was at first a fleeting and fitful notion which was limited to certain places (the highways or the justices descending on a town at the Royal assizes). During the long and generally peaceful reign of Henry III the King's peace was extended to cover the realm. A trespass action in the Royal court was initiated by a special form of *praecipe* which was not a demand but a complaint. Thus the defendant was ordered to appear ready to show why *(ostensurus quare)* they had done something wrong against the plaintiff. There were obvious advantages to this remedy especially that, since a wrong against the King was involved, the defendant could be arrested by the sheriff's officers and no *essoins* (excuses for non-appearance) would be tolerated. A fine was levied for the breach of the peace but the private plaintiff could also get damages. Such damages could then be collected as a judgement debt.

With such formidable advantages it is not surprising that plaintiffs would try to extend its uses to cover purely civil matters. Thus a drunken blacksmith who infected and killed a horse while shoeing it might be alleged that he had acted *with sticks and stones contra pacem domini regis.* Similarly it was alleged in one case that wine had been diluted and spoiled by salt water with bows and arrows, when clearly the action was in bailment or perhaps even an action in contract for the sale of bad wine. The allegation of force *contra pacem* continued to be necessary until 1348 when it was decided that it could be omitted and that the real problem could be detailed in the writ. This was done by adding to the *ostensurus quare* (to show why) at the beginning of the writ of trespass a sentence beginning with the word *cum* (since) providing the details. If it was claimed for instance the defendant had sold their goods privately in their house during a fair to avoid paying the tolls, the writ would say that "since the plaintiff has a franchise and the defendant did sell their goods privately to the loss of the plaintiffs tolls and other great harms etc. etc." and it might go on to list special rights. Since, unlike the ordinary writ of trespass, the writ *ostensurus quare cum* could give relevant details in the case and it soon became known as the *trespass on the case* or simply "case". From this point on both writs, trespass and case, existed side by side and either would be used depending on the circumstances. If there really was a battery, trespass would be used but if not then the action would be in case. There were even a number of circumstances in which both might be relevant, e.g. where a rival franchise owner was scaring traders away from a fair. In such cases the terms *contra pacem domini regis* and a *cum* clause detailing the franchise rights, would both be included in the same writ.

Trespass had been used quite early on in the fourteenth century to cover cases of professional negligence and was also used in cases where there was a public duty. In the Humber Ferryman's case in 1340, where the defendant had negligently drowned the plaintiffs horse, counsel tried to argue before the justices of the King's Bench, who were sitting in York, that since there was no sealed document nor quid pro quo there could be no action in debt, and that since force and arms had not been shown there was no trespass. The court replied that a wrong was done and that trespass would lie. Similar cases can be found where the defendant was an innkeeper or a surgeon all of which were described as common callings i.e. where a duty is owed to the general public. But these were cases of misfeasance only, where the defendant attempted to do something and failed. There was at first no remedy in trespass for non-feasance i.e. for failure to perform on a promise. However, in the fifteenth century some cases of non-feasance were allowed, mainly those where the plaintiff has suffered additional damage because of the defendant's failure to perform (rain damage following failure to roof a building in time). These were cases where the plaintiff would formerly have required a conditional bond in order to recover.

§6   *The action for deceit*

A further development of trespass on the case was the action of *deceit*. A bill of deceit was available early (1200

139

circa) in King's Bench and a writ of deceit in common pleas not much later. At first these were remedies against officers of the court or others within its jurisdiction but by the late thirteenth century this writ was being used for certain kinds of contract cases especially express warranties (the distinction between warranting and mere puffing was already clear). The action in deceit would of course lie in cases of intentional misrepresentation (fraud) but was extended in the fifteenth century to cover cases of sharp practice where there had been no misrepresentation. Thus the plaintiff could recover damages where the defendant had promised to convey property to the plaintiff and later conveyed it to a third party. In these actions it was necessary to allege both a *down payment* of money and also *disablement* i.e. that the defendant was no longer able to fulfill the contract. If they could still convey to the plaintiff the proper action would be in chancery for specific performance. A little later in the fifteenth century it was not necessary to allege down payment in the action on deceit.

In the early sixteenth century the action of deceit was said to lie if reliance had been placed on the defendant's promise by the plaintiff e.g. that he had not bought other land thinking that he had already purchased that of the defenant. Consequential damages could also be recovered. Fitzherbert's NATURA BREVIUM (1530?) records an instance where the plaintiff had given the defendant £20 to make him some carts. An action on the case was held to lie and the damages included loss of the goods which the carts were made to carry. The same result would apparently have occurred had the plaintiff merely promised payment and relied on the defendant's promise to make the carts in a certain time. In 1520 a Year Book case of Henry VIII allowed recovery in an action on the case where the defendant had not benefitted but merely promised to sell the goods to the plaintiff. St.Germain writing later in the same century (Doctor and Student) describes this as settled law.

A similar action was allowed in pure cases of debt. In a case reported in 1574 it is said "no debt is to be recovered but only damages for the debt; and this default of payment is a wrong." A promise so relied on is said to have been accepted *fideliter* (in good faith) and the defendants action as *laesio fidei* (breach of faith), both terms that we would expect to find in the Court of Chancery or the ecclesiastical courts rather than in the Court of Common Pleas or King's Bench. But this is the 16th century with the renaissance in full swing when notions of fairness and justice are in the air and when a book such as Doctor and Student, written by a supporter of the common law spoke much of justice. This tendency to consider breach of faith a wrong which should incur damages and to take reliance for down-payment is the foundation for the action on the case for *assumpsit*.

§7 The action of assumpsit

The term (and the notion of) assumpsit seems to have been imported from civil law where the risk (normally falling on the customer) passes to the contractor if they *undertake* (assume) to carry out their work in a certain manner (it is a bit like a warranty except that it is only as to a standard of care). As applied to contract in common law this meant that mutual promises (an executory contract) were thus all that was needed to create a contract and the statement is made that "every contract executory is an assumpsit in itself" *[Strangborough v. Warner* (1589).

This kind of reasoning was not at first applied to non-feasance and cases of this kind would fail if the agreement was not under seal. It was not long before the promise to pay a debt was seen as something different from and in addition to the debt, an assuming of a liability which was actionable in itself. The advantages of a trespass action (rather than debt/detinue) were quickly perceived by creditors who would try to get such a promise from their debtors. If a promise to pay the debt was obtained, assumpsit would lie in either King's Bench or

Common Pleas (debt only lay in common Pleas). When King's Bench began to hear cases other than appeals from other courts, the only writ that could be used was trespass, since it involved the King's peace. Later the Bill of Middlesex allowed King's Bench to hear other kinds of cases also but most of these were brought in an action on the case especially the action on deceit. There was some concern that where the plaintiff's case could be handled with an older remedy, say the action of debt, that the action on the case should not be used for it. However, if there was a promise to pay (assumpsit) and reliance on this promise so that the plaintiff suffered further loss, *indebitatus assumpsit* would be available. It therefore began to be alleged that the defendant, after the loan was completed, had promised to pay by a certain date and that the plaintiff in reliance on this promise had entered into other transactions to his loss. By 1573 King's Bench were overtly allowing assumpsit to be used to recover debts without express statements as to later promises and reliance (every debt implied an assumpsit) and it would seem that this had been going on for some time. Common Pleas was slower to take this route and to abandon the action of debt because oddly enough this old *praecipe* with its concomitant warranty of oath was still reasonably popular to many people and the old action of debt was still the commonest one brought in the Court of Common Pleas. The serjeants there may well have thought that they might lose business by abandoning it and allowing indebitatus assumpsit to be brought in lieu of debt. At any rate the competition between the two courts was now fierce. The banisters of King's Bench were much less expensive than the serjeants of Common Pleas and *indebitatus assumpsit* became very popular with creditors.

§8 *Slade's case*

A dispute between the two courts inevitably rose and came to a head in Slade's case (1620). Slade sued Morley on a Bill of Middlesex in King's Bench claiming that the latter was indebted to Slade for corn *which he had* contracted to purchase. King's Bench, knowing that the matter was now a hot issue, were afraid to give judgement for Slade and adjourned the matter to all the judges of England in Exchequer Chamber and it was also argued at a moot court proceeding in serjeant's Inn with Coke arguing for the plaintiff and his doughty adversary Bacon for *the* defendant. Coke, as was often *the case* in these battles, prevailed and creditors were thereafter allowed to elect between *indebitatus assumpsit and* debt. Furthermore, in the case of installment debts, it was stated that assumpsit would lie after default on the first installment whereas debt could only be brought after the time for the last payment had passed.

§8 *Implied contracts - the statute of Frauds*

The final step was taken when an assumpsit was implied when goods and services were delivered without an agreement e.g. when a traveler was fed and housed without discussion of terms and it was held that in such a case *indebitatus assumpsit* would be available. Deceit and assumpsit were still alleged in the pleadings but they could not be traversed and the action was essentially one for enforcement of a contract. This was good news for creditors and plaintiffs generally but it seemed very dangerous to many people. Anyone could come into King's Bench (or elsewhere under the *nisi prius* system) allege a debt and get to the jury on it without any written undertaking by the defendant. The result was a certain amount of backpedaling on the part of the courts and finally, in the late seventeenth century, the Statute of Frauds required special kinds of proof in a number of contractual transactions.

§9 *The requirement of consideration*

The pleadings in *indebitatus assumpsit* in addition to the promise of the defendant, laid out that it had been given *in consideration of* (here followed the details of the loan etc.). Continental courts came to enforce promises provided that they were serious promises and Canon Law used the notion of *causa* (if the defendant had a purpose or causa in view in making the promise this was sufficient to make it enforceable), but the English courts took the consideration notion and used it to distinguish those promises which were *nuda pacta* and those which were legally binding. All sorts of things might be deemed good consideration. A debt was consideration for a promise to pay, the covenant under seal implied consideration, delivery of goods or part payment for goods might all be deemed consideration. Lord Mansfield writing in the later part of the eighteenth century under the influence of Robert Joseph Pothier in France, was very critical of the doctrine of consideration. He insisted that it was only a set of hurdles established by the courts because of the difficulties in proving a contract and that these fears were misplaced since the Statute of Frauds (1677). He stated that the English law of contracts "was full of rules which no one would enact nowadays unless he were in a lunatic asylum". This argument has continued to the present day, the present mood rather favoring Mansfield and the Canonists. This may be partly attributed to the influence of American legal realism. Corbin, who was a Realist, stated that declaring that there is consideration is simply another way of saying that the contract is legally enforceable.

§10 *The development of commercial law*

Commercial law in a sense is based on contract law but is historically separate since it did not really derive from the older common law but from the law merchant which was international and based largely on Roman Law. This was developed in England in the latter part of the eighteenth century in the Court of King's Bench which assumed jurisdiction over maritime law and foreign trade. Chief Justice Holt and later Lord Mansfield adapted French and Dutch works on commercial law for use in their own court but to a large extent they were able to use the potted version of Roman commercial law produced by Bracton in the first 80 folios of his Laws and Customs. This part of Bracton's treatise was itself an adaptation of the work of the famous Canonist Ivo of Chartres whom Bracton admired.

The work of Mansfield and Holt was read in America and built upon by very learned and able judges such as Joseph Story and Lemuel Shaw of Massachusetts. The writings of these men were greatly admired in England and were in turn influential there.

§11 *The Uniform Commercial Code*

Business and manufacturing did not develop rapidly in the US until after the civil war. Oddly enough there is little sign that burgeoning business used the U.S. courts much in the latter part of the nineteenth century. This may have been partly due to the doubtful caliber of the bench during this period or perhaps to the fact that businessmen preferred to settle their own affairs by arbitration etc. The certified check appeared around 1850 and thereafter the status of commercial paper became increasingly important. Popular movements opposed making them negotiable instruments as the original people who were ultimately sued by the holder in due course were generally small businessmen and farmers i.e voters. Laws were constantly being passed to aid the little people and they were given all sorts of defenses against those who (often fraudulently) had induced them to invest in the paper in the first place. Ultimately this kind of relief, however well meant, would have strangled the development of business and some of the supreme courts in various states refused to uphold such laws.

The matter was reaching crisis proportions when the national Conference of Commissioners on Uniform State Laws was established at the beginning of the twentieth century. Their first publication, the work of John J. Crawford, was a Uniform Statute on Negotiable Instruments which was an instant success. The Uniform Sales Law which followed was an adaptation of the English Sales Act and did not have such a favorable reception. It was replaced by the Uniform Commercial Code which has been adopted in one modification or another in most jurisdictions in the US.

CHAPTER TEN
CRIMINAL LAW

§1 Common pleas and pleas of the crown

English law up to and throughout the middle ages did not really distinguish between crimes and torts. They divided cases in the royal courts into *common pleas* where the King had no real interest (e.g. a writ of right relating to title in land) and *pleas of the Crown.* The distinction is not easy to state in modern terms. It is roughly equivalent to the distinction between civil and criminal suits but that is not entirely accurate. Pleas of the Crown at first included actions such as trespass where the court might *amerce* (fine) a defendant who was found liable, as well as awarding judgment for the plaintiff. Even in common pleas the court was liable to impose fines on losing parties wherever possible. The idea of criminal law as a separate entity only slowly emerged in the royal courts.

§2 Early criminal law - the regulation of private vengeance

In Anglo-Saxon times private redress for criminal acts was still allowed although local courts of law were involved. Private vengeance was indeed much mitigated by custom. Before resorting to force there were customary procedures to be observed (quietly asking for restitution before considering force). If the defendant is in his own home and refuses to answer, one cannot break into the house and drag him out. The house must be besieged for a week or so and if he then surrenders he must be held for a month or so etc. In all but a few cases (e.g. slaying from ambush and treason) the accused could buy off the injured parties, their family or their designated avenger with a money payment which was called the *wergeld.* The earliest codes of laws that we have (The laws of Aethelred, Alfred, Canute etc.) consist for the most part of price lists governing these payments. The amount paid depended on the injury (an eye or a life or destruction of a beast or loss of property). For injuries to the person the payment also depended on the social status of the victim.

The avenger could not summarily attack his enemy on sight but had to formally charge him with his wrong. If it was acknowledged, which would amount to giving himself up, the avenger would probably take him before the appropriate court in the community where the crime had been committed. If the charge was denied this was in effect to call the accuser a liar and the matter was settled by single combat (Anglo-Saxons used the spear, Normans preferred the axe). Certain rituals followed battle. The avenger, if successful, left the body and all accoutrements where they lay, tethered the defendant's horse, drove his spear into the ground, and went to the nearest vill where he summoned the elders out to witness that this was not a murder but that everything had been properly done.

In the case of a freshly committed crime the community could be called out to find and apprehend the wrongdoer and they had no choice but to take their weapons (which were supposed to be kept in readiness for such events) and pursue the criminal at least to the county boundary. If taken red handed (in the case of murder) or hand holding (with what was stolen in their possession) or with scratches on their face etc. evidencing rape, there was no trial but customary punishment was inflicted. A gallows might be erected on the spot and they would be hanged or in the case of theft they might lose a hand or a foot. Castration and blinding were considered appropriate for rape but they might be hanged. If the accused could reach a church they could claim refuge there for up to a month. After this time they had two options; either to abjure the realm or stand trial. If they chose the former this was tantamount to an admission of guilt. Their land was forfeit to the feudal lord, their other property to the Crown and they proceeded by foot and empty handed to the nearest port where they could embark never to return on pain of death. There were certain sacred centers where the accused could stay for ever (like the cities of refuge in the Bible). These became notorious criminal nests and were abolished by Henry VIII.

If the accused escaped or could not be found they would be summoned to three successive county courts and on final non-appearance declared outlaws. All property would then be confiscated as in abjuring the realm and they would no longer be under protection of the law. Killing or maiming them would not be a crime. Outlawry for treason had to be considerably modified during the wars of the roses when taking the wrong side could condemn a whole family to poverty.

§3 *Replacement of private vengeance by official prosecutions*

Private and local vengeance was quickly altered by the strong Norman Kings. The initial change was to leave prosecution in private hands but to insist that trial and punishment should be carried out by the crown. The person accused was summoned to court, or held and brought to court by the sheriff in the case of a felony. Felony was an old word meaning wickedness or treachery and when a private accuser made such a serious charge against anyone this was called the appeal of felony. Lesser crimes were called generally transgressions and they were essentially breaches of the peace. Later these would be divided into torts (the Norman-French for transgressions) which were civil matters (though the crown retained an interest in the breach of the peace) and minor crimes which were called misdemeanors. These were punished by fine or whipping and did not involve forfeiture of property or maiming.

Private presentation of criminals was inefficient and indeed in the case of felony it was not in anyone's interest to accuse or apprehend criminals. Third parties would not want to risk trial by battle and the injured and their family would lose compensation since the felon's property would be confiscated. It was better to settle the matter privately without reporting it. The crown would of course be deprived of fines and forfeitures and private arrangement was itself declared a crime known as compounding a felony.

Early in the twelfth century official criminal presentment was introduced. Criminals caught red handed or hand holding were to be delivered over to the sheriff and held by him pending trial. Those merely accused of crimes could be held or. in less serious matters, bound over to appear.. Accusations were normally made by the men of the vill who might not be free persons. If the accused was a free man all accusations had to be evaluated by the grand jury at the county which was made up of free men. A complaint against anyone was called a bill (as opposed to a writ) and if the grand jury felt that sufficient grounds had been shown to proceed with a trial they would write *billa vera* (genuine complaint) on the back of the complaint, and a grand jury verdict against the accused is still called a "true bill".

Trials were at first held in the county court but this function was soon taken over by the Crown and all criminal trials except the most minor ones had to be tried before justices on eyre. A general eyre would of course handle common pleas and pleas of the Crown (including criminal matters). Special eyres for gaol delivery were set up specifically to handle criminal matters. The royal representative would hear the charges made by the coroners and if any vill had failed to present a crime carried out within their borders they would be amerced. If the evidence was clear and overwhelming the matter was settled and punishment was meted out. Otherwise guilt or innocence was determined by ordeal (usually by water or by the hot iron). When the church refused to allow the clergy to be associated with ordeals they lost what credibility they had. The justices in eyre setting out in 1221 were therefore instructed to decide matters in a provisional way. In clear cases, sentence could be pronounced as before. In doubtful cases where the accused was of good reputation they could be bound over but if their reputation was doubtful and the crime serious they should abjure the realm. But very quickly it became the custom to make enquiry (*inquisitio*) of the representatives of the hundred where the crime had taken place and by the end of the thirteenth century jury trial was well established. One could of course refuse it and it became usual to coerce prisoners into agreeing to "go on the country". At first this was done by imprisonment (prison forte et dure) later this was misread as peine forte et dure and the accused was tortured by placing rocks on their chest till they either agreed or died. Later again refusal was interpreted as a plea of guilty and they were sentenced.

§4 Criminal procedure

We do not know much about criminal procedure until the reign of Queen Elizabeth I (sixteenth century) but it is likely that descriptions given at this time represent a stable situation which had not changed much in two hundred years. Prisoners were brought to the bar of the court in a group shackled together by the ankles. they were then charged and the shackles removed once they had pleaded guilty or not guilty. If the plea was "not guilty", the charge was presented to the jury and witnesses, who were not sworn, could appear for the crown. Defendants had no right to call witnesses nor to be represented by counsel as that was thought to be only likely to prolong proceedings. The judge was formally the protector of the accused (still the civil law view). Cases were disposed of very quickly, in many cases in a few minutes, and the convicted felons returned to their cells often unaware as to whether they had been tried or not. Those charged with a misdemeanor could have counsel and present witnesses.

Punishment too had become less fitted to the crime. Mutilation was largely replaced by the death penalty so that the murderer was not treated any differently from someone who had purloined a small sum of money. Consequently there was no great need to list new crimes or reform the confused common law crimes, for any clarification was only likely to add one more item to the already long list of capital crimes. The system was rendered workable by discretionary pardons and mitigating the sentence of death to deportation. Deportation eventually became quite a desirable thing - free passage to a new land where there was more opportunity for a fresh start. Benefit of clergy was also used to the same end. This was originally a concession obtained by the Church from Henry II following the death of Thomas a Becket, whereby convicted clergy were handed over to the church for sentencing. But clergy did not have diplomas and it was difficult to determine whether anyone had been ordained or not. The matter was settled by offering a passage from a psalm and asking the convicted person to read it. As time went by this became in effect a first offenders act (it could only be used once) for crimes where mitigation was appropriate. An illiterate could be coached to repeat the "neck verse" and the privilege was even extended to women. Benefit of clergy was allowed in both England and America until it was made obsolete by reforms of the criminal laws. Criminal reform statutes, engineered and supported by Benthamite and religious reformers, were enacted throughout the nineteenth century in both England and America and these gradually produced something like the criminal justice system of today.

§5 *The requirement of mens rea*

Guilt (*mens rea*) was officially a necessary requirement in alleging a crime, but it was presumed in most felonies. However, some remnants of this notion persisted throughout the middle ages. A child could not be convicted of a crime if it was too young to distinguish between right and wrong. No particular age was fixed and this matter was left to the jury. Incapacity by virtue of insanity was also well recognized and automatism was at least considered in one case. The insane were only excused if they were so far mad that they did not know right from wrong and were virtually animals. The matter rested thus till 1843 when a committee of the House of Lords summoned the judges and asked their advice on this matter. The result was the McNaughton rules which were applied in the US as well as in England. The defense of criminal insanity was essentially limited by these to cases where the person did not know the nature and consequences of their act. This was no big improvement on the medieval jury instruction on insanity and the matter is still controversial.

§6 *Specific crimes - treason*

Treason was distinguished into high treason and petty treason. High treason was deemed worse than mere felony and was generally defined as treacherous usurping or challenging the King's authority. So defined, the borders of this crime were very elastic and Hale gives an instance where one was indicted for treason because he had caused another to be jailed in order to exact money from him and this kingly act was considered possible usurpation of the royal power. A statute was passed in 1351 defining treason more precisely and making it the first statutory crime. A number of items were included such as compassing the death of the sovereign or the heir to the throne and waging war against the king in his realm or adhering to the kings enemies. Edward Ward was convicted of treason following the second world war for taking part in propaganda broadcasts to England from Germany. He did not consider himself any longer a British subject but had omitted to surrender his British passport and so was deemed to have adhered to the King's enemies and hanged. Petty treason was subversion of lesser authorities as when a wife killed her husband, a servant his master or a monk his abbot. Patricide was only petty treason if the child was at the time performing services for the parent. Petty treason, like high treason, was not clergiable but was abolished and the crime reduced to murder in 1828 in England and around the same time in America.

§7 Murder, mayhem and other violent crimes

Murder (*mordhrum*) was defined as lying in wait and killing from ambush and as such was *botless* in Anglo-Saxon times (it could not be bought off) and was not clergiable. By the year 1400 it was defined by the presence of malice in the sense of malitia (bad motive) and described as deliberate or premeditated killing. Unfortunately since the death penalty came to be applied to almost all crimes, homicide was liable to be treated no differently from murder. Homicides however were divided into three kinds, malicious (which was murder and a felony), accidental deaths (which could be pardoned) and homicides arising out of a quarrel (chance medley). It came to be realized however that a chance medley, if unprovoked, should be treated as murder. Chance medley was therefore abolished and a bipartite division adopted. If the quarrel was unprovoked and the response inappropriate the death was counted a murder, otherwise it would be termed manslaughter which was a crime and punishable but it was not a felony.

Maiming (mayhem) could be privately appealed in earlier times but was not an indictable offence being simply treated as a private transgression (trespass). A number of the more serious maimings (e.g. cutting out of tongues and blinding) were made felonies in the fifteenth century. Demanding money with menaces was not a felony till 1722. There was an appeal of rape in early times when the punishment was castration and blinding. In 1285 rape was made a capital felony. Buggery was not a felony at common law as consent was presumed but became a capital felony by statute in 1533, which was not repealed in England till 1967.

Arson, malicious destruction of the property of another by fire, was always treated as a felony since the risk of spread and even a general conflagration was real when most houses were built of wood and thatched. The punishment, appropriately enough, was death by burning. However, accident was a good defense and not merely grounds for pardon. Oddly enough burning of property other than houses or granaries or even destruction of a house by means other than fire was not a criminal act. Piecemeal statutes gradually filled in the gaps and in 1971 in England the notion of unlawfully destroying or damaging property was substituted for all of these offenses including arson.

§8 Criminal entrance

Criminal entry into the dwelling of another was known in Anglo-Saxon times as hamsoken or husbrice and it was not a felony unless robbery had also taken place. No distinction between day or night was made until 1451 when burglary was defined as entering between sundown and sunrise. This distinction was drawn and burglary treated as the more serious offense since sleeping folks are off their guard and defenseless. Unfortunately housebreaking during the daytime was not a felony at all and this had to be remedied by a series of statutes in the sixteenth century. Burglary came to be defined by legal writers such as Fitzherbert as breaking and entering during the night with intent to commit a felony. Actual entry was not needed, inserting poles with hooks on them after forcing the window was burglary even though the "hooker" remained outside. Making a hole in the wall and then shooting through it was similarly interpreted as breaking and entering.

§9 *Robbery and theft*

Robbery is an offense against the person as well as property and so was a felony, at first appealable and later indictable. Mere theft (*furtum* or secret stealing) was merely dishonesty and was not at first treated as a felony at all. The term larceny (*latrocinium*) was later used to describe stealing which constituted a breach of the king's peace and which was therefore a felony. The Latin *latro* means a robber and this crime was defined by writers as taking and carrying away goods by force of arms; but the *vi et armis* requirement was dropped and the indictment would read *felonice furatus fuit* (he carried out a theft feloniously). Theft of money or goods below the value of twelve pence was called petty larceny. It was not a felony and was normally punished by whipping. Things attached to land and objects of sport and pleasure were not goods and so could not be stolen. One stern Tudor judge regarded diamonds as mere adornments to give pleasure and not goods and refused to consider their misappropriation as theft. Money other than metal could not be stolen as it was merely a promise to pay and not goods. A bailee likewise, having possession, could not be charged with larceny and a trustee who misappropriated funds to his own use was likewise in possession and so not stealing. All these loopholes were slowly stopped or at least partially occluded. A carrier was deemed only in possession of the package as a whole and so could be charged with larceny if he broke bulk but not otherwise. Similarly a servant with keys to the wine cellar was not deemed in possession of the wine. But if he was sent a distance on an errand with goods he had possession and could not steal them. Embezzlement at first meant removing arms from a Royal Armory but eventually was used to cover the acts of trustees and other persons charged with fiduciary duties. Something like modem notions was arrived at by the argument that delivery of possession to anyone was for certain purposes only and when the temporary possessor stepped outside these, their possession was terminated and they could be charged with larceny. Statutory amendments eventually created a number of categories of thefts such as embezzlement in our modern sense, fraudulent conversion, receiving stolen goods, obtaining property by false pretenses etc. Stealing in the old sense of *furtum* thus came to be treated no differently from larceny not associated with force.

This brief introduction shows how some of the notions of modern criminal law and procedure developed and how by long and tortuous historical processes, many of them not very rational, our modern criminal justice system gradually emerged.

CHAPTER ELEVEN
EQUITY

§1 *Introduction to the topic of equity in general*

The principle of equity is an old one and a simple one. Legal remedies strictly applied can work hardship in individual cases. Many legal systems arrange for a latitude which can be exercised by some official in order to ease this problem. In Roman Law this was generally the business of the praetors and in criminal matters the prosecuting attorney may decline to prosecute or clemency and executive pardons can be employed to mitigate the rigor of the law in certain cases. In the middle ages some of the borough courts and courts merchant in England had a sort of committee to dispense equity (usually with an ecclesiastic on board or someone who was learned in canon or civil law). The borough courts of York and London had such courts. Yet it is not necessary to have an additional official at all. Equity may be dispensed by the actual court hearing the case. In the English legal system equity became, for a time at least, the business of the court of chancery and this fact has left its mark on Anglo-American law. Like the Roman praetors, the courts of equity began to find that new rules and new remedies might be developed to cover the cases appearing before them. The court of Chancery indeed built up its own precedents so that equity became, not an extraordinary and occasional thing, but another set of rules and remedies distinct from that dispensed in the courts of law. These remedies and principles are now assimilated into the common law and the two are dispensed together in the same court. Yet the origins of the equitable remedies are still discernable and must be understood in order to work with them.

§2   The origins of the Court of Chancery

The Chancellor was probably the most important official in the curia of the Anglo-Norman kings. He was an administrator and chief adviser combined. The office was at first held by very distinguished prelates who had training in Roman or Canon law or both. It was only in the Tudor period that common lawyers such as Thomas More and Francis Bacon became Chancellors and by then the main guidelines and principles upon which Chancery operated had been established so that the lawyer-chancellors tended to function rather like their ecclesiastical predecessors.

When the king decided to interfere in a case, a letter was issued by the chancellor (or his office) since the chancellor was in effect the executive secretary of the king. The Latin for this is *breve* which can be translated as *writ*. As the writ system developed there came to be collections of them (registers of writs). People constantly involved in litigation, such as large landowners or religious foundations, might have registers containing several hundred writs. These would be writs in common use which would be issued by the chancery clerks as a matter of course *(de cursu)*. It was the hope of Edward I that with the issuance of new writs the whole field of law might be covered and in the second Statute of Westminster (1285) a famous clause ordered that if there was a writ covering a certain kind of case and yet in a similar *case (in consimili casu)* there was none, then the clerks in chancery should formulate one. Unfortunately when they did this the judges in the Court of Common Pleas were quite likely to *quash* the writ and so it is hardly surprising that the chancery clerks were not eager to issue new writs. C.J. Bereford in fact complained that a remedy was not available for tenants evicted from their property and ordered one to be issued which was henceforth known as the writ *in consimili casu.* During the wars of the roses the barons were zealous to maintain the common law (which they could control) and jealous of any intrusion of the chancery into law. The court of chancery was consequently rather inactive and cautious during this period. With the reestablishment of the strong Tudor monarchy this situation changed and the court of Chancery began to hear cases. Indeed the court of chancery began to prevent the common law courts from working what the Chancellor considered to be injustice, by issuing *injunctions* to the party who had prevailed at common law which prevented them from recovering.

Relations between chancery and the other courts could be a little strained at times although the chancellors generally leaned over backwards to conciliate their brothers in King's Bench and Common Pleas. Sir Thomas More when chancellor invited the judges of Common Pleas etc. (who had been complaining that chancery was issuing too many injunctions) to dinner. He offered to stop issuing injunctions if they would apply equity in their own courts in hard cases. When they replied "non possumus" (impossible) he notified them in effect that they had had their chance. Common law judges were none the less invited to Chancery to consult and advise on difficult cases as they themselves did in the court of Exchequer Chamber. The common law judges would adopt equitable notions and doctrines (in order to compete with the Court of Chancery) so that equity was infiltrating the common law at a very early stage, long before the two were merged by statute in the late nineteenth century.

§3 *The contributions of equity to common law* -

The contributions of the Court of Chancery to English law are manifold but its most important concerned modification of and development of writs. Many of these were taken over by common law courts and became part of their normal procedure.

All writs of course originated in chancery but were only effective in common law courts. However, the Court of Chancery could hear bills in cases which closely resembled writs and so, by competition, began to affect common law proceedings. The common law courts had the writs of trespass in three or four forms. The courts in chancery began to take bills in cases resembling these writs but which went beyond them in one way or another. Thus *trespass on case* was developed in chancery by the simple expedient of inserting a clause (the *cum* clause) laying out the real nature of the complaint instead of the usual legal fiction (e.g. pretending that the defendant had assaulted the plaintiff even in a case where a drunken blacksmith had injured a horses foot). The equitable origins of the action of the case can be seen by the fact that negligence must be shown, for in equity there was no liability without fault. Another trespass action known as *assumpsit* was developed which would lie when someone made a promise upon which another relied. This action was used to develop the law of contract and generally replaced the old action for debt. The writ for debt had *essoins* and *warranty* (compurgation) and so was generally unsatisfactory as a means of recovering moneys. Assumpsit did not have these drawbacks and when it was taken over by the common law courts the matter went to the jury more expeditiously. Trover and conversion were similarly actions developed in Chancery to cover cases where someone was detaining property belonging to someone else. These actions largely replaced detinue and replevin except in some parts of the United States where *replevin* (stripped of some of its common law detritus) remained a common remedy for recovery of goods. *Indemnity, an* action appropriate where an innocent person has been held liable at law for the fault of another, is an equitable remedy which made its way into the common law. Note again that it betrays its origins in chancery for the claimant must be entirely without fault since the maxim applies that *he who comes to equity must come with clean hands.*

§4 *The law of trusts.*

The development of the law of trusts is a specific achievement of English equity. There is no direct parallel to it in Roman Law though the notion of a trust is known there as it is in most legal systems. This development began before the Statute of Uses for it was in Chancery that uses were first enforced. Uses were indeed implied by Chancery where they did not explicitly exist e.g. in a sale of goods where the price had been handed over but the goods had not been delivered. In these circumstances the goods were deemed to be held on a use to convey them to the purchaser and this use could be enforced in Chancery. After the Statute of Uses passive uses were executed so that the fee (and the feudal incidents) were found to lie in the *cestui que use* (beneficiary). However, a great many uses were not covered by the Statute e.g. where the trustees had real duties, where the use was imposed on an estate other than a fee simple, e.g. a term of years or a fee tail, or where a *use* was imposed upon a prior use. The statute would not execute such uses and the common law courts refused to enforce them. Chancery therefore stepped in and developed an enormous body of law. The term use was prudently dropped and these were now called trusts.

Charitable trusts, secret trusts, implied trusts etc. are all covered by a rich body of doctrine and voluminous case law. Notable in this area are remedies available to call trustees to *account* for their handling of the trust funds. These actions became available for all sorts of situations where someone might wish to call another to show accounts. The equitable procedures, rapid and efficient, with liberal use of discovery such as the chancellor of the king could command, made these actions very popular.

§5 *The development of commercial law*

Commercial law was not really developed in the court of Chancery but it is so embued with equitable principles (due to its origins in Roman Law) that it is appropriate to include it at this point. Such commercial law as there was in the middle ages was carried on in borough courts such as the merchant courts in London, York, Bristol and the cinque ports which traded with France and other parts of Europe. In the late 18th century when commercial arrangements became complex enough to warrant it, Chief Justice Holt in the Kings Bench and his successor Lord Mansfield (with a little help from Roman Law and the first eighty folios of Bracton) undertook a great many commercial cases and developed a great body of commercial law .A little later this commercial corpus was further developed by Justice Story of the U.S. Supreme Court and then exported back to England. These materials were later used to produce the Sales Acts and the Uniform Commercial Code.

Thus although the later commercial law was developed in King's Bench and not in the Court of Chancery it arose out of an equitable jurisdiction of that court. The Court of King's Bench represented the curia regis where the King, the fountain of justice was not bound by the ordinary rules of law. In general this aspect of its activities had been lost in King's Bench as it became a regular court of common law. It remained however in Admiralty where international interests were at stake and so the king was more directly involved. When Chief Justice Holt and Lord Mansfield took over commercial jurisdiction in this court they were doing so more after the manner of the Chancellor than as justices of a common law court. The tone of commercial law bespeaks this kind of origins and thus is similar to the work of the Court of Chancery. There is an emphasis on fair dealing and equitable maxims abound. One of these is that *equity abhors a penalty i.e.* an extortionate interest forced on a needy debtor. The common law tended to allow these. Thus when Chief Justice Bereford in the early 14th century protested a penalty, the creditor, a bishop no less, demanded his pound of flesh. However, Bereford was outvoted by his colleagues and the bishop prevailed. In mortgages also the *equity of redemption* was developed i.e. a period of grace after the date of repayment had passed during which the mortgagor could make payments and recover the mortgage.

§6   *Equitable remedies*

The court of equity grew out of the *curia regis* where the chancellor was not only the executive secretary but also the conscience of the king. Consequently very swift and imperial procedures were available to the chancellor and the peculiar remedies of the Court of Chancery developed from these. The *subpoena* for instance could hale people into court on pain of instant fine or imprisonment and the *injunction* could be issued to prevent someone who had obtained a judgement in a court of law from collecting on it. If they attempted to do so they could be held in contempt and imprisoned forthwith. *Specific performance* is another equitable remedy which, like the others, is governed by equitable principles, i.e. it will only be granted when fairness and reason make it the only appropriate remedy e.g. when someone who has contracted to buy a house, if disappointed, they will not merely be injured but homeless.

§7   Procedure in equity

Proceedings in equity were intended to be less formal than those in common law courts, for one who had a complaint for the King was simply expected to come in and voice it. A writ was not necessary and an action was begun by bill, a simple statement of the complaint which could be amended if deficient in any way. Powerful means of ensuring the appearance and compliance by all parties were available and so it was rather easier to bring defendants into court in Chancery and also to obtain evidence than was the case in common law courts

§8   The maxims of equity

Equity was initially established by clerics, learned in Roman and Canon law rather than Common Law. They, and the Court of Chancery after them, tended then to emphasize principles, moral values and notions of fairness, rather than being sticklers for rules and established procedure. These principles are enshrined in the maxims of equity which in turn were largely borrowed from the *Regula* of Boniface VIII, found in the 6th book of the Canon Law. Some of these have been cited already. A typical one concerns the interpretation of wills where it is said that "equity has compassion on the (legal) innocence of the testator and wills must be construed in a kindly manner *(benigne)* so that they stand rather than fail."

§9 *Problems with Chancery and its later formal abolition*

The main problem was delay (for which it was fiercely attacked by Charles Dickens in his novel "Bleak House"). The main reason for the slowness of proceedings in Chancery was that there was really only one judge (the Chancellor). A Master of the Rolls assisted him and Masters in Chancery were later appointed, but never enough for the volume of work. This was largely cured when the Judicature Acts (1875) abolished the separate Court of Chancery and made equity a normal part of the common law. However, the separate origin of the equitable remedies can still be seen and must be understood if equitable remedies are being used. Until recently the courts in Virginia would conclude their business as a court of law and then open the court of chancery on the other side of the court room. Formal overt separation in this form is no longer necessary in open court but a similar mental exercise is advisable since actions and remedies developed in the chancellor's court still operate much as they would if they were being pleaded in the old court of chancery.

The development of courts of equity in America will be discussed in the next chapter.

CHAPTER TWELVE

ANGLO-AMERICAN LEGAL HISTORY

§1. *Time periods in American legal history*

American legal history an be roughly divided into three periods:

1.The early colonial period up to 1690.

2. The later colonial period from 1690-1776.

3, The decades following the declaration of independence.

§2 *Early colonial prejudice against law and lawyers*

The New England colonists, arriving in the new world in the early part of the 17th century, considered that they had suffered a good deal from the Established church, from powerful landed interests and from the use of law and lawyers against them. They had hopes therefore of doing better in their new surroundings and of setting up a system more in accord with reason and with their ideas (derived from the Bible) as to what was right and proper and in accord with the dignity and worth of man. It is also worth noting that they seem to have been predominantly "townies" i.e. many of them were from London or other sizable urban centers with their own courts where borough customs and law would predominate.

Negotiation and arbitration were deemed superior to law (and one of the major functions of magistrates was to arbitrate or appoint arbitrators to settle disputes between individuals.

§3 *The early colonial court system*

Within a short time, courts were set up and were at two levels. The *courts general* where everyone participated, and the *court of assistants* which consisted of the governor and his advisors. The courts general were rather like communal courts in England in a number of ways.

(i) All citizens were expected to participate and all shared (like the Anglo-Saxon *doomsmen)* in the decision.

(ii) Procedure was flexible with the minimum of formality and there was therefore no great need that anyone should be represented by a lawyer.

(iii) The ordinary business of the community was considered as well as legal disputes e.g. arrangements for maintaining roads or drains would be discussed and decided by vote.

(iv) A final resemblance to communal courts is shown by the fact that speech and general behavior were monitored so that a liar, a scold or a gossip could be punished by being put in the stocks and pelted with rubbish. This is understandable since quarrelsomeness and lying would be extremely destructive in a small close-knit community.

The court of assistants acted as a court of appeal and was also deemed to be responsible for taxation and other matters where the interests of the Crown might be involved. Admiralty and Chancery functions were thus generally the business of the court of assistants.

§4   *Administration of the American colonies from London*

When William & Mary ascended the throne of England in 1688 a new era began for all Crown colonies. Central administration became better established and relations between the colonies and the mother country became more formalized. So far as law was concerned this meant that an attempt was made on the part of the English government to ensure that, so far as this was reasonable and feasible, English law should be established in the colonies. The establishment of county courts and the appointment of magistrates to sit in them was therefore ordered and colonial law in this era tended to become more formal. Writs would be more likely to be used and the development of some kind of legal profession was thereby encouraged. Separate courts of Chancery and Admiralty might also be set up (as was done in New York) or the Governor and his advisers might act in these capacities and also as a court of appeal. The law to be administered in the courts was expected to be that of England except in so far as that was inapplicable in the colonies. The Privy Council (modern version of the Curia Regis) sitting in London heard appeals from colonial courts (the House of Lord. heard appeals from English courts). Since it was not required that colonial law adhere to English law in every particular, rules and practices would not be struck down unless they were so different and unreasonable as to be "abhorrent" to the law of England. In fact only a dozen or so such appeals from all the American colonies might be heard in any one year. A number of these had to do with inheritance (gavelkind versus primogeniture) since the eldest son might wish the privy council to declare that he should take all.

§5   *Land law in the American colonies*

One of the major differences between the colonial and English systems related to the holding and inheritance of land. In the very earliest years of the New England colonies a sort of Biblical communism seems to have been attempted but the experiment was a failure and in 1624 (or thereabouts) individual land holdings were established and rules relating to title and real property had therefore to be established. This process proceeded along somewhat original lines with three major changes from the Common Law. These were:

(i)   The establishment of a system for registering holdings.

(ii)   Rejection of primogeniture in favor of partition schemes.

(iii)   Objection to and restrictions on entailment of land.

§6   *Mandatory registration of title*

In 1624 in Massachusetts a survey of all land was ordered. Each person was to be given a *holding (approximately 50 acres) and the holding was to be registered. This* registration was to be good title against all comers except the grantor of the land. If a sale of land was not registered therefore and was subsequently regranted to someone else who did register, the second grantee, the registered one, would have good title against the first grantee. The only remedy of the first grantee would be *in personam* against the grantor (like the feudal writ *warranto cartae*).

This early land registration was necessitated by the somewhat free forms of legal documents which had developed so that a person with relatively little legal knowledge or none at all might copy a form of grant and convey title to someone else. A deed with warranty simply had to show that full ownership was being transferred and that the grantor would warrant the title both to the grantee and against all comers. The other kind of document, known as a *quit-claim,* simply stated that such title as the grantor had was being transferred to the grantee, i.e. it was good against the grantor but made no promises as to the rights and claims that other persons might have. The ease with which a deed with warranty could be made and the relative privacy of the transaction (as opposed to public delivery of seisin by turf and twig) made it possible for several people to have claim to title, and it might be difficult to resolve these rival claims.

The deeds were at first registered with a magistrate in the district where the land lay. This was not totally satisfactory for obvious reasons (the magistrate might misplace it) and it was later established that the deeds should be registered with the clerk of the county court. This strict system of land registration was not followed everywhere when land came to be bought and sold frequently as settlement proceeded west in a hurry. Quit-claims then became more common than deeds with warranty. Consequently title to land was often very doubtful especially since that most important item in a deed, (the description of the boundaries) could be woefully deficient.

A registration system not unlike that of Massachusetts known as the *Torrens system* was later introduced in a number of states but by no means in all. Even livery of seisin with turf and twig persisted long, especially in the older settlements where English forms were remembered. Land registration was only slowly established and had indeed to wait for social conditions relating to the holding of land to settle down.

§7   Opposition to primogeniture

Primogeniture seems to have been abhorrent to the American colonists from the beginning. The early settlers appear to have been used to *gavelkind* or *borough english* custom where property, including land, was equally partitioned among the sons. Daughters in the absence of sons took like a single heir as *coparceners* (copartners). This was perhaps only to be expected since the settlers (as was mentioned earlier) were predominantly from the towns and so more familiar with borough courts and customs than with the common law of the Royal courts. Their views on this matter seem indeed to have been incorporated into their initial title since many of the Crown grants were to be held as in the King's village of Greenwich i.e. in Kent where the system of gavelkind was accepted as ancient custom and therefore legal. Historians argue as to the meaning of these grants but they seem to have been interpreted in America as permitting equal partition of property on intestacy etc..

Initially the pilgrims, not surprisingly perhaps, had their own variation of partition which they based on the Bible. All property, real or personal, was treated alike and divided among the children equally save only that the eldest son was given a double portion as provided in the Mosaic law. This double portion had no good reason assigned to it (other than the authority of scripture) and so did not commend itself in other less overtly religious colonies and eventually was abandoned even in New England. The historical peculiarities of the early colonists then (their origins in England and their religious views) seem to have driven the law in this country more quickly than in England, treating all forms of property alike and abandoning primogeniture.

§8 *Fear of dynasties and prevention of entailments*

The story of the entailment of land was an entangled one in England and not indeed complete in the early colonial period. Generally entailments were held to be protected by the *de donis* provisions in the Statute of Westminster II (1285) and this statute was generally deemed to be in force in the colonies. The fee tail could indeed be barred in England but this process, whether by final settlement or collusive law suit, required some legal skill which was not generally available in the colonies. Nevertheless the fee tail maintained some kind of uneasy existence in America even in the New England states where the partition of land among the children was the more usual practice. In the south however where large estates were the rule rather than the family farm, the dynastic urge was more common and indeed more rational as the division of such estates into smaller holdings tended to make them unworkable. Entailment here was therefore common with some attempt being made to make provision for younger sons and for daughters by *inter vivos* gifts etc.

With the declaration of independence the temper of the new republic became more egalitarian and indeed somewhat hostile to any institutions or policies that were perceived as being aristocratic. English notions generally then came to be viewed with some suspicion. This trend found many advocates and may be most conveniently summarized in the views of Thomas Jefferson. The many who supported him here, envisioned the American people as a new yeomanry, with every man standing tall and independent as king on his own piece of land. From this perspective the entail was an attempt to reestablish a landed aristocracy where one person, the heir, was unduly privileged and exercised undue power and influence not only in the family but, by virtue of larger land holdings, in the community. Jefferson therefore launched a determined attack on the entailment of land and his views were influential. In New York; and in other places legislation was passed which made the entail illegal not only as to land but as to other forms of property e.g. holdings in a company.

Chancellor Kent in New York was not sanguine about the ability of such laws to control the dynastic urge which was beginning to become apparent in the city of New York and elsewhere. Entrepreneurs establishing large and successful businesses saw these enterprises as monuments to their achievements so that they had some interest in ensuring their future. These powerful persons did not indeed even need to have such laws repealed but were able to circumvent them (as their medieval predecessors did with inconvenient property laws) by means of the law of trusts.

The entail is the very embodiment of the dynastic urge and if it is considered a legitimate interest (or at least viewed as an inescapable fact of life) then the law must balance this force against other legitimate policies which (for various reasons) wish to make property as freely alienable as possible. Such has been and is likely to be the course that the law has taken and will take. Entailment of property in some form or other became generally allowed but undue tying up of property was contained by other rules such as the rule against perpetuities. However, the influence of Jefferson persisted in that control by the dead hand of the settlor was viewed with peculiar suspicion (as undemocratic). The rules against perpetuities were thus interpreted more stringently than in England.

§9   *Land considered as a national asset*

Jefferson's vision of land holding in America had one other facet, and perhaps a more important one. The great expanses of land which became available as settlers pressed westward were the property of the United States. They were used to produce revenue where possible but they were also viewed as the most important national resource and one which should be used to carry out good social policies. Land was therefore surveyed into townships (six square miles) which were each divided into 6 sections and eventually into quarter sections etc.. Grants of such land (a section or quarter section) were made on very favorable terms to encourage people to develop it and settle on it. Thus anyone who would clear the land, build a house and raise a crop could have it at a bargain price (generally 2$ an acre). Pioneer settlers were still further encouraged by being allowed to pay this off slowly and perhaps in kind, such payments being described as quit-rents. Quit rents had existed in colonial times, e.g. in North Carolina. They had proved difficult to collect and it was not easier in the case of the new grants. The settlors were voters with some political leverage and recovering the monies due was so unpopular that the attempt to collect them was in many cases abandoned. One alternative was to make the purchase price for the land payable in advance but this too had its problems. Settlors simply did not have the money to purchase the land and if they borrowed it they passed into the power of Banks and money lenders i.e. they became serfs rather than kings on their own land as Jefferson had envisaged.

Attempts were made to prevent wealthy persons accumulating large holdings but they were not always successful. Regulations forbade selling one lot and then taking another. But one who had cut down a few trees, put up some kind of a shack and raised a pitiful token crop might sell the lot to someone with ready money and start again in another state. A series of such "settlers" might therefore enable a local wealthy person to acquire large holdings at bargain prices.

§10 *Other uses of land grants*

Land was also used as a means of endowing schools and colleges, and so-called *land grant colleges* exist till this day. Railroads, to open up the country, were also given grants of land at favorable rates. As one might expect the net result of all this was not exactly what the planners had hoped. Land baronies were created and the dream of a multitude of yeomen each independent on his own holding has never quite materialized and has even faded somewhat by reason of other social forces. Industrialization and modern methods of farming have tended to move people off the land into cities and towns and to replace the small family farm with larger more efficient units sometimes (but by no means always) in the form of corporate enterprises.

The retaining of mineral rights in the land grants eventually raised a good deal of public revenue and the view that land is a national resource has remained a live policy in government. One interesting turn to this, which we will not pursue here, is the establishment of the National Parks and the development of environmental concerns and policies concerning our national resources (water, air and land).

CHAPTER THIRTEEN

CONSTITUTIONAL LAW

§1 *Strong and weak central governments*

Although the foundations of constitutional *law were established in the middle ages and* even in Anglo-Saxon times, both British and American constitutional provisions were mainly shaped in the sixteenth and early seventeenth centuries in the Tudor and Stuart periods. In the time of the Norman kings, feudalism in England was centralized and the Royal power was more or less supreme. The King was the fountain of justice and all courts, however lowly, were considered to act in his name by virtue of delegated powers. Thus *Fleta,* a book written at the beginning of the thirteenth century describes every court in the land, Royal or otherwise by the formula "the King hath his court in the (vill or whatever)". A strong King was able to ensure that this was in fact the case. Henry the Second (12th century), used the writs of *pone* and *tolt* to remove cases from the feudal courts to be heard in the county (royal) courts before the King's Sheriff.

In the fourteenth century, in the time of Edward the Third, the wars in France were waged to retain the Norman possessions there and this became more and more demanding of effort and expense. The old system of feudal levy, where a warrior was only required to fight for four months of the year, was inadequate. Professional soldiers were needed and Edward contracted with his barons to supply armies which he paid. The barons made money with these armies; they also acquired wealth in the wars by plunder and by ransoms of important people. Their troops who were termed retainers (hence the word retinue), wore their livery (uniform) and were loyal to the individual baron who had retained them. On the final defeat of the English in France these soldiers returned to England but were not disbanded and became in effect private armies. The crown had been impoverished by these wars (they had to pay the troops) but the barons often became wealthy. They then proceeded to become even richer by their control over every form of wealth in their own domain and especially by the woolen trade. The centralizing tendency of the early Norman period was thus reversed. The barons also set about acquiring all lucrative offices, further impoverishing the Crown and also generally controlling local justice, a further source of revenue. So great was their power that when the Duke of Northumberland revolted, a jury of barons acquitted him in 1404 on the ground that it was merely a private war against the Percys. Anyone in this period who wished for justice had to purchase it, as one cynic said "Men do not lure hawks with empty hands."

The Lancastrian Kings of the 14th century endeavored to save this situation by persuading the barons to join in the government by using their counsel. The words "the King hath need of counsel" were common ones in the 14th century. The council was composed largely of barons. They found the work tedious and became less and less willing to attend as time went on. This situation was not promising for central governmental institutions such as chancery and culminated in the "wars of the roses" in the 15th century. When these had ended in the late fifteenth century the barons had almost eliminated themselves as a class and they had lost any popular support that they might earlier have enjoyed.

When Henry Tudor became Henry the Seventh and ascended the throne, people were ready for a strong ruler. Henry the Seventh's council was rather different from the Lancastrian councils; there were few barons and only those strictly loyal to him, and few ecclesiastics. It was mainly composed of smaller knights who were selected for ability and loyalty. It was a small council (around eighteen in number) and many of these were not really members of the central group which met regularly with the King, but were more often on active duty elsewhere. Some became more or less permanent staff in the star chamber, some sat as judges in the court of requests (a law court specially designed to meet the needs of poor people) who could not get justice elsewhere.

§2   The tudor style of government

King Henry the Eighth (for a number of reasons) separated the English church from the papacy and put through a number of very radical changes in land law. In order to accomplish this great reconstruction he required support. In part he obtained this by redistributing church lands to favored persons but he also built up *parliament.* He used parliament as the lead horse in his political campaigns to persuade the general populace to accept his changes. This created no problem for Henry the Eighth who was a skilled persuader and a shrewd observer and manipulator of men, as was Elizabeth I his daughter. But the Stuart monarchs (who followed the Tudors) were generally less able and in particular lacked the Tudor skill and tact in handling people politically. Tudor government had generally proceeded by means of three devices.

1. Legislation. Henry VIII used legislation a good deal to attain his objectives and he was skilled in persuading parliament to support his bills. He was also skilled in drafting legislation. Sir Francis Bacon claimed that the Statutes of Henry VIII were the most perfectly drafted that he had seen. The judges were not the architects of his statutes as they had been in Norman times, though they were often consulted in the early stages when basic outlines were being formulated. The prologues to his enactments were used to state their purposes and they were very carefully phrased. These prologues relied heavily on two major arguments. The King was declared to want certain things done for the *common weal* or else he was acting in response to an *emergency.* Often emergencies were used as supporting arguments in his proclamations and statutes. These arguments may have been somewhat contrived but given the conditions at the time could generally be seen as genuine. The Tudors inherited a realm filled with violence and relinquished it to the Stuarts in a fairly stable and quiet condition.

2. Proclamations. These were executive pronouncements in emergency situations which left no time for legislation and were supposed to be temporary. So, unlike a statute, they would be discontinued when the emergency passed. There always seemed to be a crisis in Tudor times and proclamation followed proclamation. Nevertheless good historians have opined that the proclamation was not misused though it was used freely.

3. Prerogative courts. These were not seen by Henry VIIIth as permanent courts of law but rather as administrative agencies and so for the most part he set them up by executive order only. This informality was to create problems in the early seventeenth century when it was held by the common lawyers that a court must be set up either by letters patent or preferably by statute, both of which Henry omitted to do. The most important of these were:

(i) *The Court of wards* to handle the feudal incidents arising from the execution of uses.

(ii) *The court of requests.* This was set up to deal with the pleas of poor people against rich and powerful neighbors, a very necessary matter in the wake of the wars of the Roses. The masters of requests, who heard these cases, developed great efficiency for they had a lot of them to handle. It was a popular court, but Henry neglected to give it letters patent or statutory basis. Consequently, when the judges of common pleas began attacking all the prerogative courts in the Stuart period, it came under fire. Sir Julius Caesar the last master of requests said that he could not operate in any way because of the prohibitions that were issuing under Sir Edward Coke from the common law courts. Even Coke realized that the court was doing a good job and suggested that it might be regularized by a statute.

(iii) *The court of star chamber (of which more anon)*

(iv) *The court of high commission* to act *as* a court of appeal from the ecclesiastical courts (i.e. it was intended to replace the papal courts in Rome).

(v) *The March Courts*, the Courts of the North and the Courts of the West were set up to deal with turbulent border areas.

(vi) *Admiralty courts* had been established in much earlier *times* to deal with matters arising on the high seas. In 1536 by statute its jurisdiction was increased to include crimes on the high seas. The Commissioners of the Crown who presided in Admiralty were frequently common law judges and so there was no problem of jurisdiction. Later Admiralty began to hear cases originating in England which had some involvement with the law merchant or where sales over seas or property overseas was involved. This expansion of its jurisdiction was later challenged by Sir Edward Coke.

There were objections to all these courts but none were so obnoxious to the opponents of crown prerogatives as Star Chamber and its functions and operations need to be described a little more fully.

§3 Star Chamber

In 1487 a statute was passed which became known as *pro camera stellata*. This was generally believed to have established the court of star chamber so that when the latter was finally brought to an end by statute, the statute of 1487 was repealed. In fact, the words "pro camera stellata" are simply a gloss in the margin of the statute and there is no direct evidence that the court was established by this statute but rather originated in an ordinance directed at repressing bribery, rioting and so on. *But* if this statute was not the origin of the court it was directed to the same end. The court developed greatly under Cardinal Wolsey who made it his own particular realm. It became separated off in 1540 from the royal curia. The procedure began in Chancery, with a bill addressed directly to the King. Procedure, as in chancery, was largely by means of documents which were included in the record. It was aimed at repressing violence and riot and witnesses would not be too willing to come forward. Informations could be filed anonymously with the attorney general and persons fingered in this way might thus be brought in and tried in the star chamber without facing their accusers. Subpoena could be used to bring both witnesses and the accused parties into court. The sworn confession was used, the cause of many problems later on. The court had the reputation of using torture to obtain the sworn confessions but there is no hard evidence that it did. At first there was some difficulty in making defendants acknowledge the court and many of them demurred. But since the court was established in a period of royal ascendancy it was possible to compel them to attend on pain of forfeiture, outlawry, etc.. Henry VIII was generally careful to restrict the powers of his agents and to conserve the ordinary legal processes. The star chamber was intended to right those things that, due to the power of the persons or peculiar circumstance involved, were not easily handled by ordinary criminal procedure. He made it a rule that life and limb could not be punished. The star chamber normally punished with very heavy fines, which were used to express the indignation of the court at the riotous proceedings. These fines were usually diminished later drastically by as much as 90%. This process was called *taxing.* They also dealt out some unusual punishments. Thus Queen Elizabeth made juries who had brought in what she believed were false verdicts parade round Westminster with placards of a derogatory nature pinned to their chests. It is also possible that beatings were used and the American dislike of cruel and unusual punishments may be related to these procedures in star chamber.

The resources of star chamber were largely directed against riot but other matters tended to come under its aegis since its procedure was very rapid making it was thus a very effective way of controlling undesirable behavior of all kinds. Cases of defamation could be brought in Star Chamber provided the defamatory language was calculated to produce public violence. The law of libel was the result. The action in trespass *vi et armis* was greatly used and developed in this court. The Court of Star Chamber was also used to review cases where other courts were being affronted or hindered in their work by the non-compliance either of suitors or officials. It was specifically entrusted with the work of enforcing the royal proclamations and as proclamations were very frequent this represented a considerable amount of its work.

§4   *The appearance of constitutional questions*

The diminution of public unrest and the growth of stable government in the late Tudor period made it possible now to think of government by due legal process rather than by fiat. The continuance by the Stuarts of a rather autocratic approach to government which might have seemed appropriate and even desirable after the civil disorder of the wars of the roses, now appeared tyrannous. Henry VIIIth had made much use of lawyers and the legal profession was liberally represented in parliament. These same lawyers, now that times were more peaceful, began to turn their attention to constitutional questions even in the late Tudor period. These included:

(i) How does royal proclamation relate to statute?

(ii) What is the relationship of the King to the Courts of Law. Is *the King* a judge in the sense that he can walk in and sit in a court or has he only the power to set up a court? Has he even the power to set up a court without a *statute?* Has he the power to stop cases or transfer them into his own jurisdiction?

(iii) Has the Sovereign the power to *tax* or does taxation require the consent of parliament?

(iv) Is parliament a consultative body which the King can invoke or discharge at his will or is it part of the sovereign, the King in parliament?

These and other important constitutional questions were beginning to be raised at the end of the reign of Elizabeth but they became explosive under the Stuarts and a civil war was required to decide them and lay the foundations of constitutional government in England.

§5   *Cases illustrative of constitutional conflict*

A number of landmark cases illustrate the development of thinking along constitutional lines in the late Tudor and early Stuart periods.

Lane's case. This was a *case* of a franchise which was improperly issued and it hinges on whether a court of common law should accept a precedent from the Court of Exchequer. King's Bench held that it should. This emphasizes the principle that what is decided in one court should be noted as a precedent by others.

Gentleman's case. Decided in 1583 it is principally interesting on account of a long judicial dictum discussing the question of whether the King is a judge or not. The opinion of this dictum is that the King creates courts but does not sit as judge in them and there is a good deal of lament relating to the way in which the King's writs run in courts (illustrated principally by the viscontial writs (issued to the sheriff or to a local lord an beginning with the word *justicies* - "do justice"). These were not supposed to replace the feudal courts but ordered them to do justice when they had been dilatory. As to appeals it was argued that since the *de falso iudicio* only applies in courts which are not courts of record, the justicial writs are not rationing or interfering with the jurisdiction of the feudal courts.

Buckley v. Wood. Sir Richard Buckley was accused in Star Chamber per informations of being a pirate etc. These charges were not sustained in Star Chamber and so the plaintiff sued Wood for defamation. The actual decision is in some doubt since the reporting was done by Sir Edward Coke. It would appear that the plaintiff succeeded in suing for slander in the common law court but that this was reversed on appeal in Exchequer Chamber.

Bate's case. This was decided in 1606. We are now only three years into the reign of King James I and he is already in financial trouble. He inherited a £400,000 debt from Queen Elizabeth and it had soon increased to £750,000. He was advised to use import taxes which he did by royal prerogative. Bates had purchased currants in Venice for import and paid 250 pounds import duty at the ports, he then found that there was a further 500 import duty imposed by the King. He refused to pay and when the matter was brought up in the Exchequer a famous judgment was given by Baron Fleming. A statute was discussed which said that there should be no imposts without parliament but this was distinguished by Fleming on the ground that it did not apply to the King but only to the port authorities. It was said then that the King has power to regulate trade. As interpreted by Coke this meant that the King could, as being in charge of foreign affairs, reply to foreign mistreatment or imposts by in turn by taxing their imports into England, in other words that if the King was acting for the common good he could put up taxes but if it was merely to provide money he could not. The matter was ultimately dealt with by statute which said that taxation required parliamentary approval. When this was discussed in parliament in 1610 Whitelock in his speeches put forward and emphasized the view that there should be no taxation without representation, a point that was not lost on the American colonists later.

§6   *The Court of High Commission.*

Henry VIII felt obliged to take the serious step of a break with the papacy for a number of reasons not least of which was a sense of disillusionment and disappointment over the decision of the Pope in the case where he had sought to have his marriage with Catherine of Aragon anulled. Catherine had been betrothed, which in those days was the same thing as marriage, to Henry's older brother who had died. Henry, who was a theologian (he had indeed written a monograph refuting Martin Luther and been named defender of the faith by the Pope) was somewhat uncertain of the legality of his marriage. When he had numerous stillborn children and only daughters but no sons to secure the succession and keep England from civil war, he began to feel that he was living in sin and that this was God's judgment upon him. He was personally fond of Catherine and apparently in no way desirous of divorcing her for any other reason. When the pope, who was more or less the prisoner of Holy Roman Emperor Charles the Fifth (Catherine's nephew), decided against him for political reasons Henry was disenchanted. He later came to believe that the Canon Law was obscuring scripture and the breach with the papacy was initiated.

186

Other factors began to enter in. Henry and many Englishmen objected to the ecclesiastical drain on the wealth of England. A great deal of land was in frankalmoign and as such contributed nothing to the realm but did contribute by ecclesiastical taxation to the papacy. Likewise the ecclesiastical courts were greatly weakened by the readiness and ease of appeal to Rome and also the frequency and rapidity with which cases were taken out of local jurisdiction. When Henry "nationalized" the English Church and its lands and assumed the position of defender of the faith and head of the Church of England he had to replace and strengthen a weakened ecclesiastical law system. His purpose was not to abolish this and substitute the common law. He wanted the supervision of faith and morals that was exercised by the ecclesiastical courts to act as a moral and theological undergirding of law and society. The ecclesiastical courts had been weakened and had no sanctions other than spiritual ones, which in the current temper of England seemed not very effective. The Court of High Commission was Henry's response to this problem and he typically established it in a somewhat casual way. There were no letters patent and there was no statute. The commissioners functioned simply as a part of Henry's curia. Their business was heresy, salus animae (spiritual health) family law, wills, contracts, and generally things dealing with faith or good faith. The system was complicated with archdeacons courts, bishops courts, provincial courts, etc. but the ultimate appeal was now to the High Commission. The latter as a royal commission had powers that the ecclesiastical courts did not have. The High commissioners freely issued subpoenas and punished with fines and imprisonments. Letters patent were issued by Mary and in the first year of Elizabeth a statute established the high commission.

In the early stages it was supervised by the council and staffed for the most part by non-ecclesiastical judges. Later it became related to the ecclesiastical administration and in 1587 Archbishop Bancroft was placed in charge of it. From then on it was mainly governed by an archbishop, the last being Archbishop Laud. It became independent around Bancroft's time, began to establish its own licensing of proctors and attorneys and used precedents. The precedents advocated by Bancroft were not only those of the court itself but also precedents in ecclesiastical law. The court also handled a good deal of business that we would consider common law and tended to handle it rapidly. There is an interesting quotation of Elizabeth's where she urges it to conduct their business in haste. Consequently, since it was speedy and reasonably cheap there was a tendency for it to increase its business and compete with the common law courts, which of course roused their resentment. This was ultimately voiced by Sir Edward Coke and is similar in that respect to the resentment against the other prerogative courts.

§7   Objections to the Court of High Commission

Controversy concerning the High commission centered round two or three matters.

(i)   Tithing j

(ii)   Jurisdiction

(iii)   Procedure.

In the matter of *tithing,* the arrangement was that the State collected the tithes or tenths of everyone's income and with that administered the church, paid the salaries etc. Thus people who did not agree with the established Church were obliged to contribute to it, and this created a good deal of resentment among the puritans. Hostility to the established church on the part of the puritans was brought over by them to the New World and incorporated in the US constitution. The Church of England was not disestablished in England until the 20th century and remnants of the establishment still remain (the monarch must be a member of the Church of England).

In the matter of *jurisdiction* the common lawyers felt that the operations of the High Commission were removing too many things into the area of ecclesiastical law. They appealed back to the precedents of Henry the Second when he was battling with the church. At that time a compromise (the Constitutions of Clarendon) was achieved with the help of a famous canon lawyer, Azo of Chartres. It was laid down there that the decision whether a matter is ecclesiastical or common law is a matter for the common law to decide.

As to *procedure* the usual sequence of events was that informations were lodged or the court proceeded even without them. Informations might be anonymous. A person accused was haled into court and there took an oath. This oath was to tell the truth, the whole truth, etc. It was only after the oath that interrogatories were addressed to the defendant, which had to be answered under the same oath. Following judgment by the court, those convicted could be fined or imprisoned. Imprisonment was also used for contempt of court. The *oath ex officio* was a deadly weapon against the puritans whose conscience would not allow them to lie. Also when interrogatories were put to lay persons asking their opinions on certain documents, it was very easy to trap them into a statement which might be judged heretical.

§8 Attacks on High Commission by common lawyers

An early case, in the time of Queen Elizabeth I was *Smith v. Smith* decided in 1600. Here a wife was haled into the Court of High Commission accused of adultery by an information lodged by her husband. In order to bring her to court a writ of *capias excommunicando* was issued and the court officers broke down the door to arrest her. It was declared in the Court of Common Pleas that the court had no right to issue a capias to bring someone to court. This is similar to the decision in Ball's case which was quoted earlier. In 1607 (the same year as Nicholas Fuller's case) a discussion was held in the sergeant's inn after dinner. There the status of the High Commission was discussed. It is interesting that one of the arguments made was the following:

Either the high commission is founded by letters patent or by statute. If by letters patent, the sovereign does not have the right to interfere with the common law or its courts. If by statute, the common law can be altered but since the prologue of the statute of the first year of Elizabeth suggested that the act was restoring an ancient royal right, it was interpreted as therefore not abrogating common law.

With this cunning argument it was declared that neither a capias nor any other writ could be used to bring anyone into the ecclesiastical court and that life, limb, goods and land could not be taken without a recourse to common law courts. Since goods included money the ecclesiastical courts could not even fine. It is also remarked in these cases that no layman can be examined under oath for heresy, that the only examinations of laymen under oath would be for the ancient cases of marriage and wills, both particularly belonging to the ecclesiastical courts. It was also said that no one could be interrogated without knowledge in advance of the articles in which they were to be questioned, also that no one could be asked about secret opinions concerning what they said or did.

Nicholas Fullers case, was decided in 1607. Nicholas Fuller was an attorney representing the Quakers who constantly challenged the jurisdiction and the procedure of the Court of High Commission. His manner was so vigorous that his conduct and language were said to be scandalous and he was held in contempt and imprisoned. A discussion was held in Exchequer Chamber on a writ of consultation. The case was decided in Fuller's favor and following this an open attack on the Court of High Commission was made with the common law courts issuing writs of prohibition and habeas corpus to free any persons imprisoned by the Commission and deciding matters in their favor in King's Bench. It was also held that if there were any part of any one of the counts which related to a matter of common law then the entire case should be decided in a common law court.

These measures took away from ecclesiastical courts the right to bring someone into court and also the right to punish them in any way even by fine. It left them with only the ecclesiastical sanctions such as excommunication so that Canon Law was more or less inoperative and ecclesiastical control of morals and orthodoxy was completely undermined. This situation was temporarily halted by removing Sir Edward Coke from the common pleas.

Roper's case. Roper held a piece of real property charged with the payment of a pension to a clergyman and declined to pay it. The matter, probably an ecclesiastical affair, was nevertheless settled in the common law courts in Roper's favor.

The importance of all these things is that they contain the germ of discussion of such matters as relationships between executive government and the common law courts, the right to private opinions and weight to be given to the interest of the State in security and in maintaining views (e.g. patriotic ones) which contribute to and may be bound up with the welfare of the state. These matters were greatly discussed among the Puritans, many of whom were lawyers, and the impact of these discussions in the new world must have been very great.

§9 *Coke's arguments with King James*

On the 10th of November 1608, Coke took part in a consultation with the King known as *the case of prohibitions.* In this discussion the archbishop declared that it was clear in divinity that the King himself may intervene and decide any case. Coke replied that the King as the fountain of justice must only proceed by appointing judges. He is not even the judge in his own courts but the judgment is given by the court. This is an interpretation of Fleta's statement that "the King bath his court in the county etc., etc." Statutes quoted for this proposition were mostly from the reign of Edward the Third or Henry the Fourth. It need not surprise anyone that statutes restraining the King from exercising judgment on his own were from the period of the Wars of the Roses when the barons were powerful enough to control the courts. At the end of this discussion there was some mention of a case where the King had given a sentence about a controversy over land. The King stated that law is based on reason which the King surely has. Coke replied that it is artificial reason which requires long study and experience, and adds that this artificial wisdom, this thicket of the Law, protects his majesty in safety and peace. The idea that he was protected by the law instead of the vice versa apparently threw the King into great wrath and Coke states that he then quoted Bracton that "*rex non debet esse sub homine, sed sub deo et lege*" (that the King ought not to be under any man but under God and the Law). Note that other versions of this episode give a more craven picture of Coke, notably the account of Sir Julius Caesar the master of requests.

This double version of Coke's behavior may not be completely contradictory. Coke may well have feared for his life from the successors of the Tudors; but his resolution may nevertheless have been strong and in one of these discussions when all the judges are on their knees pleading for mercy Coke apparently continued the argument "from the floor." Usher, a contemporary, stated that on November 14th, four days later, Coke issued a further prohibition and this is a case where the offender was clearly guilty. The statute of the first year of Elizabeth establishing the High Commission stated that it had power to reform errors and heresies. The term reform was interpreted strictly by Coke in this case, excluding from it any action attacking life, liberty and property. In other words he leaves the ecclesiastical courts with no remedy except exhortation and perhaps excommunication. Should this interpretation fail he also says they are only empowered to treat *offensa gravia*, great offenses. This is very suspect from the statute where the phrase "offensa gravia" is probably added as an additional task of the commission. In all these discussions, Coke insists that letters patent are not able to change the common law and that the King, by letters patent, cannot make a crime where none was before. So since letters patent cannot allow the commission to attack a man's life or property, except in common law courts, and since Coke interprets the statute so that this cannot be so, there was no power left to the high commission, and the entire administration of ecclesiastical law fell into abeyance. This was probably a bad thing as a great area of the law of wills and contracts was left unenforceable or poorly enforceable, and further the important moral and doctrinal support of the Church was greatly weakened. Note, however, that although prohibitions continued to issue after 1610 they were very few and the ecclesiastical courts were able to function reasonably well after that time.

§10 *Commissions of enquiry*

These were originally merely methods of acquiring information but began to be used to refer cases which turned up during their enquiries to be heard in prerogative courts. This procedure was very offensive to Coke for a number of reasons.

(i)   The proceedings were by English bill. This did not mean that he objected to the language but to the fact that they were informal rather than being presented in the fixed formal way of pleadings.

(ii)   *The commission's* charter was doubtful. Its proceedings were only authorized by a schedule annexed to a statute.

(iii)   People's reputations could be damaged without remedy by such summary procedures. This point we have seen raised before in connection with Star Chamber when an accusation of piracy was made.

(iv)   Perjury was a very simple matter, easily raised in these procedures and one for which the defendant had no remedy.

(v) Coke objected to the interpretation of the statute of the fifth year of Elizabeth which established these commissions.

It would appear that there were some grounds for Coke's objections as a good deal of perjury is believed to have gone on and in some cases people of good reputation were attacked in a clandestine manner by their enemies.

Sir Edward Coke also delivered prohibitions against the activities of other prerogative courts such as the Court of York (a court of equity) in some of which he argued that a new court of equity could not be produced without a statute. The old Court of Equity existed by ancient custom.

§11 *The case of the royal proclamations*

Royal proclamations had been used freely in the reigns of the Tudors and a discussion between Coke and the lords and the King's ministers was set up to clear the air on this topic. Coke argued, as we would expect, that the royal right of proclamations was incompetent to change any part of the common law or statute law or the customs of the realm. This contention was based not surprisingly on the statute of the time of Henry the Fourth. (wars of the roses). He also insisted that the *King* cannot create any offense by a proclamation that was not one before for "ubi non est lex, ibi non est transgressio" (no law, no wrong) and added that an act which is not legally wrong cannot be punished. There is some discussion as to what the King may do to prevent dangers which it would be too late to prevent afterwards and which might aggravate the offenses which were afterwards committed. In effect Coke is contending that the King should not be able to use the royal prerogative to create law. Here again the King continued to use royal proclamations and to back them up in Star Chamber. This stimulated parliament to produce a petition in the year 1610. It would seem from this that the King had been using proclamations freely to enjoin as law something that had been specifically rejected just a few weeks earlier in parliament.

In the matter of the proclamations, as elsewhere, Coke was temporarily defeated; the battle passed into parliament and these matters were finally dealt with by the act of Settlement in 1701.

§12 *King's right to discuss pending cases with a judge*

Peacham's case was decided in 1615. Peacham was a politically active rector and had written a sermon expressing his belief, common among the puritans of the time, that the King would be smitten from on high as Ananias in the book of Acts. King James is reported by Coke to have been greatly distressed by this to the extent of hiding in his chamber. Since the accusation was not founded on Peacham preaching the sermon, but by its being discovered during a house search, there was some constitutional difficulty about pressing charges against him. The King in this difficulty wished to consult with the judges privately one at a time so that Coke could not influence them. Coke rejected this proposal absolutely stating that this was tampering with the judges. Finally he did give an opinion but it was hostile to the crown. In 1616 Coke's career as a justice of the King's Bench came to an end when, in the *Bishop of Lichfield's case,* known also as the *case of commendams,* there was a dispute about the royal ability to appoint clergymen to certain ecclesiastical livings. The King, being involved, asked Bacon to write to Coke requesting that he delay his decision till the King had spoken with him. Coke reiterated his former opinion given in Peacham's case. He was dismissed for refusing to give an opinion in advance of judgment. Note the fine statement in Coke's third institutes, "therefore the judges ought not to deliver their opinions beforehand upon a case put and proofs urged on one side in absence of the party accused, especially in cases of a high nature and which deserve so fatal and extreme punishment.-- For how can they be indifferent who have delivered their opinion beforehand, without hearing the party, when a small addition or subtraction may alter the case."

§13 *Dr. Bonham's case - courts set up by Royal charter*

This famous case was an action for false imprisonment brought against the president and censors of the College of Physicians. These, under a charter, issued licenses to practice medicine in the area of the city of London. Dr. Bonham, who held a degree of doctor of physic from the university of Cambridge but who had failed their oral examination, was forbidden to practice. He insisted on practicing and was fined five pounds by them and to be under pain of imprisonment if he continued to practice. He had a writ of prohibition issued and it was decided by Coke and his companions that the charter, even though statutory, did not give power to imprison or to fine, interfering with goods or body. Since then the college had no power, the situation is reached, as Lord Ellesmere remarked, "that leaving such liberty to empiricks within the city of London they may practice pell mell without restraint or fear of imprisonment which both the patent of Henry the Eighth and the act of parliament does suppress." The important point in this case is not the matter of the prohibition but the handling of the statute which established the college. This statute was set aside on the grounds that it required something that was unreasonable, this being that *someone should be judge in his own case.* A number of cases were cited in Bonham's case, in one of which the mayor of a city, who also happened to be the officer of its court could not claim statutory establishment of his court since it enjoined that he be judge in his own case. The wording of the dicta in the case is very wide and some interpretations of it have suggested that any unreasonable statute could be overturned by the courts. In the later case of *Godden v. Hales* in 1686 (during the restoration) the same doctrine was used to show that such statutes as took away the Kings prerogative were illegal as the Kings prerogative to do what he liked was part of the law of the land and was reasonable. The sword of Bonham's case can cut both ways. The matter continued to be debated for some time but we can see that by the 18th century, when Blackstone wrote, the accepted position is that the authority of parliament is supreme so that the judge can hardly overturn it; but, of course, he can presume that parliament would not wish to produce some extremely unjust, harsh or obscure measure. The judge might then feel free to take the offending clause in some more humane or reasonable sense. From Bonham's case arose the rule of statutory interpretation that acts of parliament are to be strictly construed where they change common law or interfere with life liberty and property.[*Note the discussion in US of judicial review of legislation*]

§14 *The conflict with the Court of Chancery*

Coke's struggle with Chancery was partly legal partly personal. He had very strained relationships with Ellesmere, the Lord

Chancellor. The nub of the dispute concerned the removal of cases from common law courts by Chancery after judgment had been given. The legal arguments involve precedents. Those from the 15th century, favored by Coke, suggest that a case cannot be removed from one court by another. Those from the times of the Tudors, favored by Ellesmere, show a great many Chancery injunctions being upheld. One can use case to support either of two different interpretations of law by selecting the period in which the cases were decided. In addition two statutes were invoked; first the *statute of praemunire* 1535. This statute forbade any person to be dragged from the realm into a foreign court or for judgments to be rendered abroad on matters to do with the realm or that one should go from one court in order to bring to nought or impeach the judgments of another court. Coke interpreted this to mean that "the parties ought to remain quiet" after judgment was given in any common law court of the land. He completely ignored the fact that this had not been interpreted in earlier years so as to prevent the Chancellor from considering a case after judgment had been given. Bacon, in his discussion of this statute, makes it plain that the statute was intended to attack ecclesiastical courts which were reviewing common law courts and to attack persons being indicted to appear in Rome, or cases about English property being decided in the ecclesiastical courts outside the realm. All of these measures were widely considered in England to involve great injustice. The other statute cited in this controversy was *the statute of prohibitions* likewise probably irrelevant to the argument.

§15   Coke interfering with equitable relief in Chancery

Courtney v. Glanvil was decided in 1615. Glanvil, a rascal, sold a number of jewels of very little value to a young buck. He made the sale easy for him by having it warranted by one Hampton for 600 pounds; the total value was probably 10 pounds. Courtney then sued Hampton for the money by collusion, had the matter appealed on a writ of error into the Kings Bench where the judgment was upheld; thus the case was collusively judged and appealed and yet Courtney was robbed. Coke applied for habeas corpus and released Glanvil. *Sir Moyle Finch's case* was quoted in argument.

This was a case where one Throgmorton, who had leased land from Queen Elizabeth, was guilty technically of being late with one rent 21 years before the reversion was purchased by Sir Moyle Finch. On finding this technical default Finch declared that the term of years was void and ejected Throgmorton. In strict law this is correct but was hardly equitable. Nevertheless, because judgment had already been given, Coke held that there was no equitable relief, and the writ of error had been used here to make judgment doubly certain. Also quoted was *Cobb v. Moor* from the time of Edward IV. Moor, who was out of the Kingdom, was defrauded by a collusive action for debt in his absence. Again a writ of error was used to make the common law appeal complete and no relief apparently was given at that time. Notice that this was in the time of Edward the Fourth when common law courts were strong and the chancellor's court weak. Note also that the cases cited by Coke's opponent Bacon tend to be from Tudor rather than Lancastrian times (i.e. when the King was strong).

§16 *The rest of the story*

Coke was dismissed in 1616 and entered parliament as a member of the house of commons where he was instrumental in drawing up the petition of rights. This was never passed into law but has been much cited in constitutional discussion ever since. Its major themes include the following:

(i) Taxation must be authorized by statute.

(ii) There should be no enforced loans with special oaths being sworn (used by the King to raise ship money).

(iii) Protestants have the right to bear arms in order to defend themselves.

(iv) Troops shall not be quartered on the civilian population in time of peace.

(v) Martial law shall not be declared or applied in time of peace.

Many of these items are substantially included or even quoted verbatim in the first eight amendments to the US constitution. This is hardly surprising for when we study the law libraries of the gentlemen of the American colonies we find that the two most commonly found law books were *Coke's institutes,* with their interpretation of Magna Carta and various other statutes and Coke's abridgment of his case reports etc. The consequences of Coke's influence has been a great emphasis in the US on the importance of the jury, a great emphasis on the due process of law, (interpreted somewhat differently than by Coke), annexing taxation to statute and very strict restrictions upon special administrative proclamations. Note the right to bear arms and its rather peculiar antecedents in English political and legal history.

§17 *The interpretation of Magna Carta*

Magna Carta became *the symbol of civil* and religious liberties both in England and in the United States. Its most cited provisions were
:

(i)   The Church should be free.

(ii)   No one should be deprived of life liberty or property except by the law of the land and the judgement of his peers.

(iii)   Justice should not be sold, denied or delayed.

(iv)   Taxes should not be imposed without consultation with the notables and representatives of the realm (the precursor of parliament).

(v)   Property should not be taken by the Crown without compensation.

(vi)   The right to travel freely both in England and abroad.

There were also provisions relating to the use of foreign mercenaries to impose unpopular government on English people and clauses prohibiting blocking important commercial waterways by fishing weirs. These were interpreted by later writers as implying the right to bear arms and the principle that one could go and trade wherever one wished.

Magna Carta was seen by Coke as an unrepealable enactment which established for ever constitutional government and the civil liberties implied in it. Later writers, such as the late Sir Winston Churchill, have described it as an expression of the interests of the barons rather than the common people and treated it moreover as a statute just like any other which could be and has indeed largely been repealed. Cynical acid has also been used to make the point that "judgement by ones peers" could not refer to jury trial which had not been invented in 1215.

It is worth noting, however, that the draftsman of Magna Carta was not one of the Barons but the Archbishop of Canterbury, Stephen Langton, who was very much concerned about the common people. He was also the driving force behind its enactment, urging the barons to stand up to King John and on occasion having to face the King and his army alone, armed only with his office and a good deal of personal courage.

It is also worth noting that the decision of all the suitors present in the customary courts (the judgement by ones peers referred to in Magna Carta) was similar in principle to jury trial. It ensured that decisions about life limb and property were ultimately in the hands of the ordinary people not officials of the Crown.

For a good discussion of Magna Carta and its later influence see A.E.Dick Howard's ROAD FROM RUNNYMEADE.

CHAPTER FOURTEEN
THE LEGAL PROFESSION

§1. *Pleading in early customary courts*

Lawyers did not exist as a class in the Anglo-Saxon era nor indeed for some considerable time after the conquest. The vill, manorial and early county courts resembled a town meeting rather than a modern day court. Someone involved in a legal proceeding in one of these "courts" could, and often did, bring a companion to support and assist them. It may be also that some such friends (like Dendin in Rabelais' "Trial of Judge Bridlegoose") achieved some reputation and made or supplemented a living (a chicken here, a bag of corn there) as counsel, in this primitive sense of the term. The earliest Royal courts likewise had no need for professional lawyers. The eyres and assizes were not much different from the communal courts, a sort of free for all presided over by a Royal justice. With the development of forms of action and formal pleading, expert guidance became important and a legal profession slowly began to emerge.

Formal pleading, as e.g. we see it in Hamo's case in the early thirteenth century, consisted of formal recital of a claim in court by the plaintiff, and formal denial of this claim, point by point, by the defendant. This procedure was called *narratio* (narrating) in Latin and *counting* in Norman-French ("conte" meaning a story) and so has nothing to do with mathematics. The counts in a plea might be numbered (count 1,count 2 etc.) but each was a little story and lawyers have been telling little stories ever since. As procedure hardened and became more formal it became important to get the story right and professional narratores/conteurs (or counters) became the first English lawyers. It has also been suggested that the hardening and formalizing of the writ system contributed to the professionalization process in another way. Proceedings in a royal court consisted of discussion aimed at bringing the pleadings to an issue which could then be decided by some means or other (ordeal or jury decision). This was done by bringing the cause of action within the four corners of the appropriate writ and then deciding whether the requirements (elements) of that writ had been met. Once committed to a course, it might be difficult or impossible to change it, e.g. starting out with a general denial it might be impossible to enter a special plea. It has been suggested that one of the important functions of the professional counter was to carry out the preliminary fencing (licking the plea into shape) without committing his party to any particular line. At the critical stage in the proceedings (when the plea was about to be entered into the court roll) the counter would therefore consult with his client, a process called *avowal*, and only after avowry was the client committed. The term attorney arose to describe this practice and this relationship between counsel and client.

§2   The serjeants-at-law

In the latter part of the thirteenth century a special and prestigious class of counters begins to emerge, these were called *serjeants.* The original of this term is the *serviens* or squire who accompanied the knight in battle. Servientes (later the army sergeants) acquired a form of military tenure in land called serjeanty. It has been suggested that larger landowners aed religious corporations attached some of the abler of the narratores (counters) to their establishment by grants of land in serjeanty, an estate which carried homage and fealty. Be this as it may, these serjeant-counters acquired a great deal of importance, prestige and wealth and eventually came to be ranked with the great nobles of the realm.

§3   Provisions of Edward I for the licensing of lawyers

Edward I, the English Justinian, took some critical steps in directing the future of the legal profession. In 1292 a royal writ was sent to Meetingham C.J. and his fellow judges, enjoining them to provide and appoint (ordain) a certain number of the better and worthier attorneys and the more promising students of the law, and that only those so chosen should follow the court and no others. Here is the formal entrustment of the license to practice into the hands of the judges, a system that has been maintained in common law countries ever since. Edward I also made the first royal appointment of a serjeant making William Herle (later a capable and important judge) a *serjeant-at-law* by means of a royal writ issued in 1310. (This by the way is not the direct origin of King's counsellors, the senior group of the British Bar, but resembles that institution greatly). According to Sir Edward Coke this step meant that Herle was the king's serjeant or servant; and the tradition has become established that lawyers even when they are representing private persons are carrying out a function of the court itself, they are the servants of the court and so of the state.

In taking these steps Edward I did several things.

(i) He began the professionalization process for lawyering, since formal selection of the best students as apprentices will inevitably become linked to measures to train and educate them.

(ii) He prevented admission to the legal profession from becoming a family matter as it did in Europe, a feudal tenure of legal serjeanty that would normally be inherited like any other estate. Licensing was linked to ability not to family.

(iii) Legal education was also linked to the practice of law rather than being located in the Universities as it was in Europe. University law professors in England taught foreign law (Roman Law and Canon Law) not the common law of England. The Viner chair of Law in Oxford, established in the eighteenth century, was the first University chair of English Law (Blackstone was its first incumbent). Until that time the universities and legal profession went their separate ways. The lawyers by the way considered their educational arrangements superior to those of the universities and for a time they were.

§4 The inns of court

The inns of court were initially simply the hostelries where the serjeants and apprentices dined and discussed their business. Soon however they became virtually law schools with formal lectures and set moot arguments (a difficult issue in law thus became known as a moot point - one suitable for argument in a moot court). The instruction was not done by the serjeants, they were too important to teach- but by the "great apprentices" who by then were nearly as important (they were put in the same taxation bracket as the serjeants and major landowners). Social instruction was considered as important as formal legal studies and music, dancing etc. were included as essential parts of the curriculum. The inns of court were thus social centers for youth and the children of notable families would be sent there as to a finishing school even if they were not intended to become lawyers. Ultimately this social aspect of the inns became rather predominant and the inns of court acquired the reputation of being sinks of iniquity and schools of vice in the eighteenth century (generally a century of great moral decline among the nobility and landed gentry).

The masters in the inns (who were normally apprentices) supervised the instruction and there was a governing board of *benchers* who supervised the running of the inns. Benchers of course might and often did lecture (Francis Bacon gave his lectures on the regula (maxims of the law) and on the Statute of Uses when he was a bencher. From time to time the masters would recommend a student for promotion and this took place through various stages. At the top of the profession were the serjeants, then the apprentices who could practice outside the bar in the court which enclosed the clerks and students. They were thus known as utter (outer) banisters. Within the bar were the students and those who were not yet admitted to the distinguished level of apprentice. These were known as inner banisters.

§5   The court of *King's Bench and the order of barristers*

To escape from the confines of the inner bar took ability and probably resources. To rise from apprentice to the rank of sergeant certainly took money. The creation of a sergeant took about seven days and involved feasting of his colleagues, distributing liveries, gold rings and other gifts all around and generally spending money like water. A large group of lesser lawyers, like lesser clergy, developed around the legal luminaries of the outer bar in the Court of Common Pleas. These made their living as best they could but eventually established themselves as top ranking lawyers in their own right in the court of King's Bench. In the 14th and 15th centuries courts began to compete for business. The fiction of the Bill of Middlesex enabled the court of King's Bench to try cases relating to land as well as trespass, their own specialty. This expanding legal business of the King's Bench needed lawyers and the supply came from the outer banisters of the Court of Common Pleas. The term barrister to describe the senior branch of the English legal profession, derives from this move. The serjeants indeed declined thereafter though the title lingered till 1877 when the serjeants inn was sold.

§6 *Solicitors and their hold on legal business*

The profession now had a central group of court room lawyers who were professionally trained, at least in the technical aspects of law. Their practice was very much oriented to the courtroom and they would not normally confer much with their clients. Their preference was rather to form some idea of the nature of the case and proceed to battle it out in court in accordance with the science of pleading, their specialty. Inevitably there grew up around these men a second outer group, persons with some knowledge of law who could be approached by someone needing legal help. It was from this group serving the barristers that the solicitors arose.

At first solicitors were no more than brokers for the barristers, but they gradually increased their preserve, acquiring eventually the exclusive right to see clients and initiate legal proceedings. With this came their own provisions for the legal education of their pupils. For quite a long time this took the form of apprenticeships in a law office splemented in time by instruction and examinations..

It came to be the rule that banisters could not directly be hired by a client nor indeed talk to a client except in the presence of their solicitor. The true law offices were now those of the solicitors. Banisters collected themselves in chambers as a matter of convenience but did not form partnerships. A number of them would simply occupy a set of chambers and share a law clerk who could be contacted by solicitors who had briefs to confer on the barristers. The barrister in short argues the brief provided by the solicitor although a conference with clients could be and usually was arranged. Interviewing of potential witnesses by the barrister (in the presence of the solicitor) could likewise be arranged if necessary.

§7   Current relationship between solicitors and barristers

The original division of the legal profession into two groups banisters and solicitors, was like a rigid caste system, the two existed side by side but, like oil and water, they never mixed. This system has become modified considerably over time. Barristers can and do specialize in office practice, doing conveyancing, probate or commercial work and seldom if ever going to court. Solicitors on the other hand have increasingly sought and obtained court room privileges, at first in petty courts but now being allowed to appear in the high courts under certain circumstances. This division of the legal profession into solicitors and barristers has been viewed and admired by many American lawyers as being like he division of he medical profession into generalists and specialists. But It is clear that this division of the English legal profession is nothing like the distinction between general and specialist practice in medicine. It is the product of commercial competition between professional interest groups (clubs if you like) which has gradually been altered to provide a relatively workable legal system. Proposals to abolish it continue to appear periodically though up to this point they have not succeeded. The arrangement is currently under review. It is indeed conceivable that it will be abolished and that British lawyers of all kinds will be able to form partnerships and specialize among themselves according to their taste and training (more or less on the U.S. model).

§8 Other types of legal professional

Some other professional groups emerged and persisted for a time in England and several of these are still important in Europe.

Scriveners were originally clerks who copied out legal documents. They gradually acquired the right to execute documents on their own, especially those relating to debts and mortgages. As such they required a somewhat evil reputation and despite efforts to expand it, they were confined to this area of the law and eventually abolished. *Notaries,* still important in France, tended to draft wills and such documents. These too have virtually disappeared In Anglo-American legal practice, although the name persists in the office of the notary public. The ecclesiastical and admiralty courts, and also the court of chancery, had licensed practitioners of their own called by various names (the ecclesiastical lawyers were called *proctors).* All these were abolished in the reform legislation in the latter part of the nineteenth century. A uniform system of courts was set up and the English legal profession divided into only two categories, banisters and solicitors. The ecclesiastical courts retained only jurisdiction over internal matters relating to the church. If the ecclesiastical courts require the services of lawyers, which is only occasionally the case nowadays, it is usual to employ lawyers from the secular courts. These may be given the (temporary) title of proctor etc..

§9 *The appointment of judges*

Judges, as the justiciars or representatives of the Crown, were and are still appointed by the British government as are Federal judges in the United States. Such appointments therefore have tended to be and often have been political, an arrangement which was less than ideal. Eventually judicial appointments were made from a short list presented by the bar. Judges of the high court level and up in Britain are always knighted, a practice no doubt stemming from the ancient classification of distinguished lawyers with the nobility. All judges of this rank and higher are addressed as "my lord" (m'lud for short) and the highest group of judges, those who function in the House of Lords and in the legal proceedings of the Privy council, are called law lords and titled Lord Smith of (whatever town or locality they choose). No British judges are elected as many judges in American State court systems are. Each system has its advantages and disadvantages and the questions as to the best method of judicial appointment continues to be debated and proposals of various sorts put forward.

§10 *The development of the legal profession in America*

In colonial America there was at first a great suspicion of lawyers, but gradually they made their appearance and a number of the sons of good family would be sent to London to live and study at the Inns of Court in London. Whether they learned much there is open to question. More than one parent complained that they learned little law and much vice (for moral standards at the Inns were not high).

Americans have always been somewhat ambivalent in their views about the usefulness of lawyers and the necessity or even desirability of lawyers in order to work the legal system. A number of attempts were made in the early colonies to prevent a lawyer class from emerging but never quite succeeded. It was at one stage a crime in Georgia to attempt to practice law and *at* least one person was fined for doing so. However, lawyers established themselves and indeed distinguished themselves by the notable part they played in the independence movement and in writing the US constitution.

Training for the legal profession until modern times was for the most part by way of office apprenticeships, although a Chair of Law was founded here and there in the newly developing colleges. Some law offices became specialized in teaching apprentices, the *Lichfield School* being the most famous example. Lectures were given and practical training provided. Great judges and writers were produced in this way. Indeed, in the first half of the nineteenth century the American judiciary achieved an eminence that has hardly been surpassed anywhere[8]. American legal writers during this period were also considered among the best in the world. The work of Joseph Story on commercial law was particularly admired and his writings were read in England and influenced the law of sales there.

---

[8] Distinguished American lawyers followed their own, very stringent, patterns of continual legal education; rising early and reading foreign classical legal texts

With the development of the American west and the inpouring of immigrants into the eastern states in the latter part of the nineteenth century, a different picture emerges. Standards for admission to the bar were almost non-existent in many places; a few questions asked while having a drink with a judge in a bar was often the extent of it. However, in the last quarter of the nineteenth century the university law school began to make its appearance, the American Bar Association was founded and legal education and training began to take the directions it has maintained since..

ILLUSTRATIVE DOCUMENTS

DESCRIPTION OF MOOT PROCEDURE AS CARRIED OUT AROUND 1660

The new barristers are, for their degree, to perform each of them two several assignments of moots: which exercises are done in the hall in the term-time only, every Tuesday and Thursday night immediately after supper. The case is framed with apt and proper pleadings unto it by the two utter barristers who are to perform the assignment. These pleadings are recited by two gentlemen under the bar, one of which speaks for the plaintiff, the other for the defendant, which done, and the case briefly put out of those pleadings, and argued by the utter barristers, three of the benchers as judges argue the same case ... [And in these moots] the benchers proceed as followeth. Immediately after supper the benchers assemble themselves in the bay window at the upper end of the hall; where standing in order according to their antiquity, there repair unto them two gentlemen under the bar whose turn it is to recite the pleadings. Who, after a low obeisance, demand whether it be their pleasure to hear a moot, and depart with an affirmative answer. Then the benchers appoint two amongst themselves to argue the case, besides one of the readers elect ... When it is appointed who are to argue, all the benchers depart out of the hall, leaving the rest of the company there. The two arguers walk a turn in the court or garden until the hall be prepared and made ready for them; which being done, they return into the hall and stay at the cupboard, demanding if the mootmen be ready. (During their stay at the cupboard there is oftentimes a case put unto them by one of the utter bar...) But to return to the mooting: all parties being ready, the two benchers appointed to argue, together with the reader elect, take their places at the bench table, the ancient bencher sttling in the midst, the second on his right hand, and the reader-elect on his left. Then the mootmen also take their place, sitting on a fom close to the cupboard and opposite to the benchers. On the one side of them sits one of the students that recites the pleading, and the other on the other side. The pleadings are first recited by the students, then the case put and argued by the barristers, and lastly by the reader-elect and benchers, in manner and form aforesaid; who all three argue in English, but the pleadings are recited and case argued by the utter barristers in law-French. The moot being ended, all parties return to the cupboard, where the mootmen present the benchers with a cup of beer and a slice of bread; and so the exercise for that night is ended   .

SPECIMEN OF A MOOT COURT PROBLEM

Someone siesed of certain land has issue two daughters by different mothers and dies; a stranger intrudes and leases to the younger daughter for life; she leases over to her sister for term of her life [in mortgage] on condition that if she pays certain money at a certain day she shall have fee, and if not that [the elder daughter may enter and hold [in common] with her; at the appointed day she does not pay, and so they hold in common; the rent is behind, the lord distrains, the two daughters make replevin; the lord avows, and they disclaim; the lord brings a writ of right upon disclaimer and recovers by default; the lessor brings a writ of entry *in consimili casu,* recovers by default and leases to the younger daughter, against whom the elder daughter brings a writ of mort d'ancestor; the assize is taken by default and she recovers and dies without issue; the younger daughter enters; the lord brings a writ of escheat against her. Someone siesed of a certain piece of water which is divided between two counties aliens half the water (with a spring) to a man and the other half to a single woman; (the alienees] marry each other, the husband and wife alien the wife's land to someone to hold of thm by homage, fealty and the [services of] twenty shillings, and they have issue; the husband dies; the woman, reciting the former grant confirms the tenant's estate, to hold of her by the services of five shillings; the woman dies; the issue enters and aliens the water to someone to hold of him by the services of finding him as many nets as he needs for fishing (on reasonable notice being given) and that he might fish in the water at his will; the issue dies; the alienee aliens half of the water, as far as the middle line, over [to someone in fee]; the paternal uncle and the maternal uncle find a boat on the water and an ox in the land, and take them; the others make replevin. *Ceux que droit.*

CHAPTER FIFTEEN

LEGAL LITERATURE

§1. *The Anglo-Saxon period* .

Legal literature prior to the Norman invasion consisted of statutes, charters and local court reports. The statutes were largely criminal in character; but they are not nor are they intended to be comprehensive. They only contain the Royal modifications of the law of the land e.g., fixing the fair amount of wergild to be paid for each offense. Charters establishing *book land* were generally documents presented by hopeful grantees to prospective grantors for their approval. As such they were often works of art, modelled on whatever precedents the author could find and embellished with phrases borrowed from continental sources. Few court reports have survived but some of these, being the work of ecclesiastics, are quite sophisticated. The manorial court of the Bishop of Ely for instance kept quite elaborate reports of its proceedings.

§2 *Early Anglo-Norman literature*

The *Leges Henrici Primi* (laws of Henry I) represent an attempt of an unknown author to summarize the state of English law in the early part of the 12th century. It gives the coronation charter of Henry I (it was usual *for a King to proclaim his good intentions and* policies on this occasion). The remainder of *the book is* commentary on the various bodies of customary law then extant in various parts of England, with cross references to Civil, Canon and Frankish law. The legal situation must indeed have been confusing after the conquest and the author was trying (perhaps not very successfully) to make sense of it - for what kind of readership one cannot be very sure. However. it has been described by Maitland as the first English law book. About the same time the *Laws of Edward the Confessor* was published, again by an unknown author. This is a frankly nostalgic work which is anti-Norman in its tone and harks back to the good old days of the Anglo-Saxon kingdoms. Much of what is recited as ancient law is believed to have been fabricated by the author. Yet It was taken very seriously in the seventeenth century when legal antiquities were beginning to be collected. Sir Edward Coke e.g. regarded it as an ancient and accurate source and used it as materials for his attacks of the prerogatives of the Crown.

§3. *The late twelfth century*

Two important books were published in the latter part of the reign of Henry II. The *Dialogue of the Exchequer* was written in 1117-1179 by Richard Fitz Nigel Bishop of London, who was in charge of the office in that period. It is a detailed description of the procedure by which the crown managed its accounts and how hearings were conducted. A little later the famous treatise bearing the name of *Glanville* appeared. This is not likely to have been written by Ranulf de Glanville himself (a great judge and statesman of the period). It has been suggested that his illustrious nephew Hubert Walter, Archbishop of Canterbury was the author. It represents indeed the emerging common law of the King's court and as such is a slim and simple volume in a radically new form. It consists of a description of the royal writs then available and commentary upon them. It was soon obsolete of course but continued to be used and some attempts were made to update it from time to time. The most famous of these rewrites was produced in Scotland and known by its first words *Regiam maiestatem.*

§4   *The plea rolls*

The records of the various royal courts were carefully kept almost from the beginning. However, they were not law reports as we know them but more like minutes of the proceedings. They did not contain any record of arguments but only noted pleas made and that judgement was entered for one party or the other. The arguments made and the reasoned opinions given were of course important but they were, at this early stage, preserved in the memories of the lawyers and judges concerned. When a case is cited as a precedent in the year books there is often a lively discussion between attorneys and the bench as to what was actually said on the earlier occasion.

The first plea rolls were the great pipe rolls of the Exchequer which have survived and which demonstrate a continuous record from 1156 till 1832 when the court was abolished. The early rolls of the Court of Common Pleas and of Kings Bench are thought to have been diaries of the students but soon became minutes of the proceedings taken by the clerks and as such were not made available to the parties or their attorneys. The lawyers at first had no control over what was written but it soon became customary to remain off the record while the pleas were being licked into shape. When it was time to go on record the judge would warn the attorneys who would then measure their words very carefully and so have a fairly precise notion of what was being entered into the record. Finally the lawyers authored the pleadings themselves and had them approved by the court and entered in the rolls. Bracton, as a distinguished justiciar, was able to obtain possession of the plea rolls and *used* them extensively in preparing his treatise on the laws and customs of England.

§5   *Bracton's treatise*

Bracton's treatise is the first great English law book and it is still very readable. Henry de Bratton was (like his predecessors and teachers Martin Pateshull and William Raleigh) an ecclesiastic, eventually becoming Chancellor of Exeter Cathedral. He was employed as a Justice in Eyre and of the King's Bench but did not apparently sit in the Court of Common Pleas. He ceased writing around 1253 either because the Chief Justice had demanded the return of all court rolls in his possession (the principal resource that he used in his writings) or because the struggle between the barons and the King had interfered in some way with his work. However, he did not take sides in this affair. Like many of the great judges during the later wars of the roses he remained aloof and attempted to keep law separate from politics.

There are two parts to his book. The first 80 folios (about a quarter of the work) are prefatory and were intended apparently as an introduction to law in general rather than English law in particular. A good deal of the material in this part is based on Roman or Canon Law and covers topics, such as bailment and other commercial items, which had not come before the common law courts in England. The second and main part follows the pattern of Glanville and considers the forms of action, one writ at a time.

The notable feature of this part is the extensive use made of case reports from the plea rolls. Bracton had apparently borrowed these precious items and even entered marginal notes in them directing his clerks which parts they should copy. The note book which resulted and which he used in the compilation of his treatise was discovered in the late nineteenth century by Sir Peter Paul Vinogradoff.[9] To Bracton indeed we may owe the extensive preoccupation of English Jurisprudence with case law and this part of his work appears to have been very influential at the time, to judge from the number of other writers who imitated him. But Bracton was no idolatrous worshipper of cases and his jurisprudence, as revealed in his practice, has no resemblance to that of Austin. His cases illustrate how judges applied such law as there was to the cases which appeared before them and Bracton is very free both with praise and criticism. Much of the criticism is reserved for the judges of his own day whom Bracton believed to be very inferior to his masters, Pateshull and Raleigh. The cases which he cites are indeed usually about twenty years old since he probably considered the more recent ones to be unworthy of comment.

The first or introductory part of Bracton may have been read with interest but could hardly have been important at the time of writing since English commercial practice was not developed to the point where the Roman Law discussions had any real application. However, this part of Bracton turned out to be most useful eventually when Chief Justice Holt and Lord Mansfield were developing commercial law in the English common law courts during the eighteenth century. By then, commercial practice was becoming sufficiently complex to need the procedures of later Roman Law and the first eighty folios of Bracton's work was available as a handy summary of these valuable and now apt legal materials.

One little sentence in Bracton proved to be most important where he described the King as not being subject to men but being under God and the law (*sub deo et sub lege*). Sir Edward Coke was to make good use of this phrase in his constitutional disputes with James I and

---

[9] Russia émigré, a distinguished historian who was elected to a chair in Oxford in the nineteenth century.

the separation of the legal and executive functions has become a firmly established constitutional principle both in England and in the United States.

§6 Imitators of and commentators on Bracton

A number of writings generally imitating or otherwise based upon Bracton appeared in the latter part of the thirteenth century. The most important of these were two books which appeared around the year 1290, which are called Fleta and Britton. They appear to have been written in an attempt to bring Bracton up to date in view of the extensive legal activity of king Edward I. *Fleta* (written in Latin) is most famous for his treatment of the court system which reflects the tremendous extension of the Royal influence in this direction in its formula "the King has his court in---". This expression is used to introduce every type of court, communal or royal. The King is considered, by this author at any rate, to be the sole fountain of Justice. All legal proceedings and all courts derive their authority from the King and their officers act as his representatives and surrogates. *Britton* on the other hand.(written in French) takes the form of a Code and professes to have been written by the authority of the King. It is indeed possible that this is so for Edward I contemplated an extension of the common law writs that would be comprehensive and not merely supplementary of the law administered in communal courts. *The Statute of Wales* (contemporaneous with the Statute of Westminster II in 1285) indeed purported to be such a code.

§7 Other early treatises - the Mirror of Justice

A number of less important treatises were also composed in this period. The *Summa* (summary of the law) of Sir Gilbert de Thornton C.J. is one of these . Very interesting and most curious is the *Mirror of Justices,* also composed about 1290. Andrew Horn the chamberlain of the city of London and custodian of its records is believed to have been the author and it is a great mystery how this serious antiquarian, or indeed anyone else, could have come to produce this work. It is very critical of contemporary law and harks back to the golden age of the Anglo-Saxons. Since the author had no knowledge of the law of this earlier period the work is largely fictional. It was apparently unknown during the middle ages but was printed in the 16th century and taken very seriously by Sir Edward Coke as evidence for the proposition that the King was not in ancient times above the law.

§8 *The Year Books*

The Year Books began to appear in the reign of Edward I and continued until the middle of the sixteenth century (1260-1535). They then yielded to law reports produced by private persons under their own names. There is some dispute as to the origins of the Year Books. The earliest of them e.g. those dating from the reign of Edward II are available in several versions clearly prepared by different persons. Later they become uniform and apparently more official. Prof. F.S.C. Milsom's[10], view that they represent, at least in the early days, the court notes of the students, has much to recommend it. Those of the reign of Edward II (1290 -1310) are particularly interesting as they were produced during the great flowering of the serjeants-at-law, and for the most part record their exploits. They contain a little gossip about them, record their witticisms and even note their absences by reason of illness. They were at first written in Norman French, later in Latin and finally in English. They were used as contemporary practice manuals and so apparently only the most up to date ones, covering recent years, were used. Even with the invention of printing only recent numbers appeared in print. However, by the middle of the sixteenth century printed year books covering most of the three hundred years of their history were available. Sir Edward Coke studied these works intently in his efforts to determine the constitutional status of law and the relation between Law and the Crown. His great hope was to take these medieval precedents and apply and develop them to meet contemporary needs ("from these old fields must come the new corn").

---

[10] Baker and Millsom, EARLIEST SOURCES OF ENGLISH LEGAL HISTORY

§9 Practice manuals

These include manuals on pleading called *narrationes* and collections of forms called *books of entry*. Registers of writs need to be mentioned as they were important practice manuals for lawyers until comparatively modern times. New writs were produced from time to time and it was always possible for a lawyer to ask the court to issue a new writ; but well established ones were issued "per forma" and compilations of them would be kept by individual chancery clerks and also probably as reference works by private practitioners and ecclesiastical foundations. Writers such as Glanville probably used such registers as the source and basis for their legal commentaries. But later more or less official registers were available; and writs which did not conform to the local official version might be quashed.

§10 *Littleton and Coke*

The first great law-book to be written since the time of Bracton was Littleton's TENURES produced in the second quarter of the fifteenth century i.e. during the earlier part of the wars of the roses. English land law had by then become extremely complicated. The original feudal estates with their rents and incidents had been hopelessly confused by the efforts of landowners either to sell or grant their land to third parties or to prevent this from being done. Littleton, a serjeant at law and later judge of the Court of Common Pleas, sorted through this complex and confused mass of materials and was able to reduce it to a very rational and readable work. His treatise has three parts. Part I discusses the various estates in land, Part II the feudal incidents and Part III special doctrines such as co-ownership. Sir Edward Coke greatly admired Littleton's Tenures and used it as the basis for the first part of his Institutes which became known indeed as *Coke-upon--Littleton*.

§11 *Fortescue*

Around the same time that Littleton was producing his work Sir John Fortescue, in exile in France with the house of Lancaster (red rose), produced two works, the most famous of which is a short treatise *In praise of the laws of England*. This consists of a dialogue with his pupil, the young prince Edward, in which Fortescue sought to instruct him in his duties as a King. Particular emphasis is placed on the importance of a general knowledge of law in one who would rule a country. The work compares the laws of France (rather unfavorably) with those of England and even the language of that country is considered inferior to the French of the Year Books. Fortescue had pondered deeply on the proper functions of law and government during his exile and the work reads well today. In general he is an advocate of a limited monarchy and his work was of course used against king James I, by Coke.

§12   Doctor and Student

About 1523 Christopher St. Germain, a barrister, published a dialogue between a Doctor of the Civil Law and a student of the common law known as *Doctor and Student*. This was written first in Latin but an English edition was published in 1530. This work was written at a time when there was a great revival of Roman Law studies and many countries were "receiving" some form of civil law as the law of the land. A reception of civil law to replace the Common Law was indeed being strongly argued and later used as a threat by Henry VIII to persuade the lawyers in parliament to support his radical policies.

LIST OF IMPORTANT DATES AND EVENTS

400-600 a.d. Roman Britain ended 406 a.d. (barbarian invaders had crossed the Rhine and the legions were being recalled to defend Rome). Britain became divided into a number of separate kingdoms which were gradually overrun by Angles, Saxons and Jutes from Scandinavia who had been invited to come as allies by one of the embattled English kings and thereupon gradually took over the country. The difference between the English and the Scots has been explained (by the latter) as a mathematical matter, the acute angles turned north and the obtuse angles turned south. The replacement of the old British kingdoms by Anglo-Saxon ones took about 200 years to complete. With the arrival of Augustine in Canterbury in 597 a.d. the christianization of the Anglo-Saxons was begun and proceeded apace until the old Norse gods were a forgotten memory. The Anglo-Saxon king Aethelred produced the first Anglo-Saxon code of laws. King Alfred of Wessex used the Danish invasions in the 9th century as a means to unite the Anglo-Saxon kingdoms into one. He also produced a body of laws which was named for him. However, the Danish invasions continued and half of England was wrested from King Alfred in 879. The Danish King Canute (Cnut) united England under his control and and ruled England, Norway and Denmark (1016-1035). He too produced a significant body of laws (the laws of Cnut). He is said to have placed his throne before the incoming tide to take down his flattering courtiers who said that the waves would obey him. He did not, as some students have averred, introduce Danish pastry into England.

Edward the confessor (1043-1066) was childless and appointed William Duke of Normandy his heir. The English thanes however elected Harold according to the Anglo-Saxon custom - hence the battle of Hastings where Harold got an eyeful of arrow and William of Normandy got the crown of England. The Anglo-Norman period lasted till the reign of Edward I (1272-1307) by which time the two populations had become indistinguishable and spoke a language which was neither Norman-French nor Anglo-Saxon but English.

William I(The Conqueror) 1066-1087 had the Domesday Book compiled.

William II (his son) 1087-1100. Westminster hall built.

Henry I (his nephew) 1100-1154 *Leges Enrici Primi* (?1113-1190) the first attempt at an English lawbook

Glanvill wrote his commentary on the writs in 1187

Richard I (the lion hearted) 1189-1199

John 1199-1216. Action for attaint in plea rolls 1200

Magna Carta signed 1215

Henry III (son of John came to throne aged 9) 1216-1272

Hamo's Case decided 1220-1221

Bracton wrote around 1254

Provisions of Oxford 1258

The Great Parliament 1265

Edward I 1272-1307, great legislator who brought Vicarius to Oxford from Italy to teach law (he did not invent Vicarious liability), directed the production of a number of important statutes including Statute of Wales (intended to be a complete civil code), Westminster I in 1284, Westminster II in 1285 and the Statute of Mortmain in 1290. The *Year Books* had their origin under Edward I. The Model Parliament met in 1295. Edward also made arrangement for the training and appointment of lawyers following the court.

Andrew Horn wrote *The Mirror of Justice* in 1290.

Fleta and Britton (updating Bracton) written around 1290-1292.

Edward II 1307-1327. Common Law was developing rapidly. Year Books flourished. Nisi Prius system established but facts settled by local juries. As a result the action of trespass began to be used extensively and to be developed for uses other than battery. Edward II was deposed by parliament in favor of his young son (Parliament was being used as a tool by Queen Isabella and her lover Roger Mortimer).

The reports of the Bishop of Ely's court at Littleport held in 1321 recorded.

Edward III 1327-1377 Black death 1348-1349 Peasants revolt 1381. Serfs then become scarce (and valuable) and their lot improved so much so that they got a rush of blood to the head and revolted in 1381. This was crushed but their conditions continued to improve to the point that their form of landholding (copyhold) was so well protected that holders in fee simple used legal fictions (John Doe and Richard Roe) in order that their holdings could be treated in the same way. The fee simple and copyhold became identical in the seventeenth century (when the American colonies were being settled).

Richard II 1377-1399 The Merciless Parliament of 1388 met. Parliament forced Richard to resign in favor of Henry IV.

Henry IV 1399-1413 First king of the House of Lancaster, and the first irregular succession in 200 years. For the next century, the rival York and Lancaster families contended with each other for the throne in the *wars of the roses* which ended in 1485 with Henry Tudor taking the throne of England. Many important legal and political changes were made by the Tudors.

Henry V 1413-1422 The second Lancastrian King

Henry VI 1422-1461 The puppet king, taken to all the battles of the wars of the roses, like a mascot, by whatever party had him in custody at the time.

Christopher St. Germain 1460-1540. His most famous writing, *Doctor and Student* first published in Latin in 1523. Later published in English in 1530.

Edward IV 1461-1483, Yorkist monarch, six feet four inches tall, a soldier who never lost a battle and a trader who never missed a deal (he became very rich)

Littleton's *Tenures* written in fifteenth century, described as the first great English law book since Bracton's.

Littleton died 1481.

Sir John Fortescue's *In Praise of the Laws of England* 1470-1471.

Edward V (1483), one of the little princes murdered in the tower i.e. the *wars of the roses are* on again.

Richard III 1483-1485 (wicked uncle of the little princes)

Henry VII (Henry Tudor of Wales) defeated Richard at the battle of Bosworth field in 1484 and reigned 1485-1509.

Henry VIII (bluff King Hal) reigned 1509-1558. He separated the English Church from Church of Rome, abolished military tenure converting all military estates to socage (non-military) tenure. He was a great legislator, the Statute of Uses and Statute of Wills drafted by him created great opportunities for legal development and reform which however were not taken up by the common lawyers so that Chancery had to take up the challenge and developed a considerable legal corpus known as *equity* which was incorporated into the common law in the late 19th century in England while in some American states it lasted as a separate body of law into the twentieth century.

1535 The *Year Books* end, replaced by *The Reporters.*

Dyer's Reports 1537-1582

Elizabeth I 1558-1603 Colonial expansion and struggle with Spain culminating in defeat of Spanish Armada by

Sir Frances Drake in 1588. The Writ of Mandamus became an official writ in 1573.

In the reign of Elizabeth international trade expanded which necessitated the development of international law especially commercial law which is associated with the name of the great Dutch jurist Hugo Grotius. The developing body of trading custom was systematized in the late eighteenth century by Chief Justice Holt and Lord Mansfield in England and in the early nineteenth century by a number of distinguished American lawyers especially Justice Lemuel Shaw in Massachussetts and Chief Justice Joseph Story. This commercial legal corpus was the basis for the Sales Acts in England and America which was later revised in the US to become the Uniform Commercial Code (UCC) [original text 1951]

Plowden's *Commentaries* 1537-1582

Coke's *Reports* 1572-1616

John Selden 1584-1654. Historian interested in ancient documents. The Selden Society, founded in his honor, publishes old legal documents and books e.g. *The Mirror of Justice.*

William Prynne 1600-1669

Sir Matthew Hale 1609-1676

James I 1604-1627

Slade's Case 1602.

Dr. Bonham's Case 1609

Charles I 1627-1649. Civil war broke out in 1642, parliamentary forces finally victorious by 1649 when the king was executed.

Coke's Institutes voi1 1628, vol.2 1642, vol.3 1644, vol. 4 1644.

Parliamentary rule 1649-1660 (Oliver Cromwell)

Charles II. Stuart monarchy restored 1660. The restoration period was notable for a considerable reaction to puritanism which was seen in the theatre and literature generally (restoration comedies were generally naughty). Notable legal events in this period were the Statute of Frauds (1677) requiring all transactions relating to land to be in writing.

Charles' son James II officially converted to the Ro¬man Church during his reign and began to appoint Catholics to prominent positions. Fears about an attempt to reestablish "popery" in England emerged which culminated in the "Glorious revolution" of 1688 when parliament invited Mary the elder daughter of James to assume the throne. Mary who was a protestant insisted that she share the throne with her husband Prince William of Orange, Stadtholder of the Netherlands, and so they reigned together as William and Mary. William and Mary (mostly William) stabilized government and legal arrangements generally. He established the Privy Council to deal with colonial affairs, including legal appeals, and encouraged colonies to develop their own adaptations of the laws of England i.e. only those hopelessly at variance with English ideas of justice would be overturned. His soubriquet "Good King Billy" does not however derive from his reestablishment of the protestant faith in England nor for his generally good and wise administration but from the fact that he abated the Stuart tax on beer.

The Duke of Norfolk's Case 1681 first suggested the Rule against perpetuities.

Sir William Blackstone, (1723-1780). Commentaries (1765).

Burrow's Reports (1756-1772) (introduced a new standard for reports).

The American Declaration of Independence 1776

The Constitution of the United States 1787

The Federal Judiciary Act of 1789 establishing the Federal Court System in the United States.

James Kent's Commentaries on American Law 1826

Christopher Columbus Langdell 1871 published his casebook on Contracts and so went public with his new concept of legal education.

The American Law Institute began the Restatements of the

Law 1923-1939 as well as beginning to formulate the Uniform. Statutes.

Edward II 1307-1327. Common Law was developing rapidly. Year Books flourished. Nisi Prius system established but facts settled by local juries. As a result the action of trespass began to be used extensively and to be developed for uses other than battery. Edward II was deposed by parliament in favor of his young son (Parliament ws being used s a tool by Queen Isabella and her lover Roger Moimer).(.